I0485563

COLORING BOOK FOR ADULTS

FAVORITE FLORALS

WHO ENJOY GARDENS AND FLOWERS

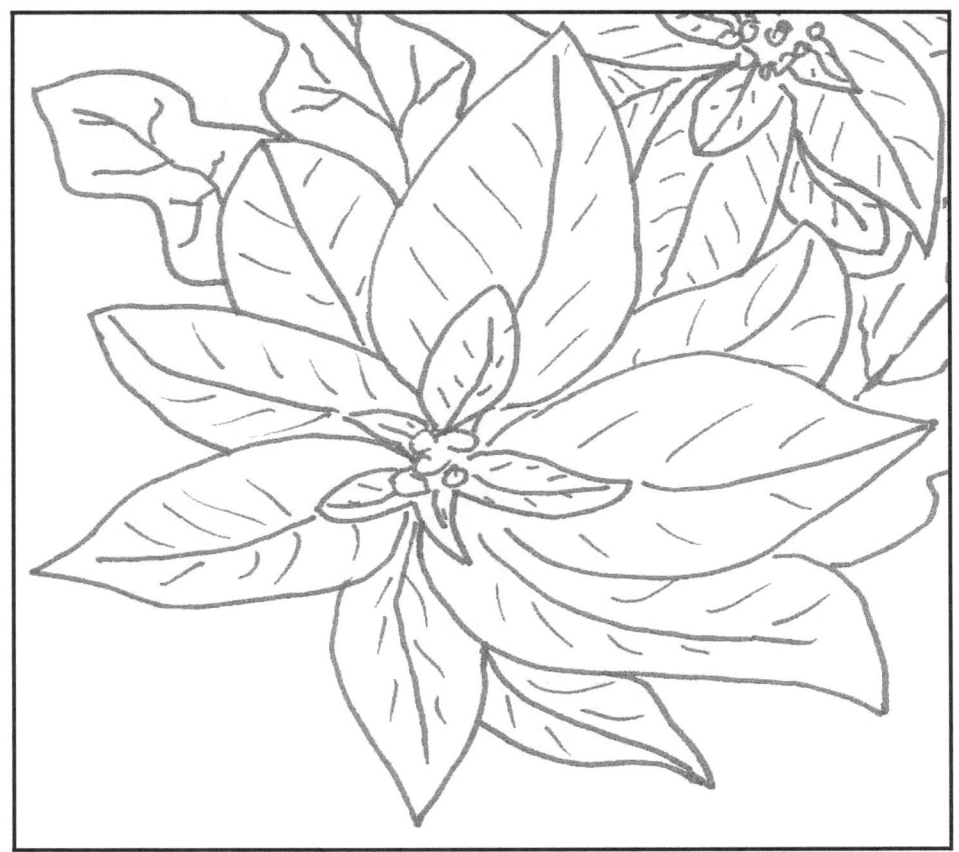

By Kaye Dennan

KD Coloring Studio

ISBN-13 978-1518800597

PUBLISHERS NOTES
Disclaimer

All Rights Reserved. No part of this publication may be reproduced in any form or by any means, including scanning, photocopying, or otherwise without prior written permission of the copyright holder.

Copyright © 2015 KD COLORING STUDIO

Paperback Edition

Manufactured in the United States of America

Kaye Dennan

A note from the Illustrator

When it comes to coloring most people like to color flowers and trees at some stage throughout their experience. This book brings to you a wide range of floral images to enjoy your coloring hobby.

Discovering your inner artistic pleasure is one of life's happiest moments. It is a creative experience you can enjoy all on your own but one that you can share with others as well.

When you start coloring it is easy to color between the lines and find enjoyment just in the practice of adding color to paper.

As you continue in your discovery you will find that colors talk to each other, they mix and blend and create new emotions.

Colors speak to us too.

Become aware of the affect of colors on your emotions. Take the time to site and understand the change of emotions as you take in colors that you see. When outside look at different colors and recognize your emotion. Look at blocks of color and see if it makes any difference to the way you feel.

Most of us have favorite colors and they are favorites because we like how they make us feel when we see them or even wear them.

Some people even find that their observance of a color a person is wearing affects the way that they initially react to a person: positively, negatively or cautiously.

Basic relationships are listed below but the reality is that what might make one person feel cheerful can make another person feel irritated depending on the viewers' past experiences or cultural differences.

KD Coloring Studio

Warm Colors – Red, Orange, Yellow

Cool Colors – Green, Blue, Purple

Neutral Colors – Black, Gray, White, Tan, Brown

I encourage you to experiment with color and shapes and enjoy your coloring pass-time.

****

Every Second Page has been printed with a repeated design so that you do not ruin one of your colored designs with bleeding.

Hibiscus

Copyrighted Material

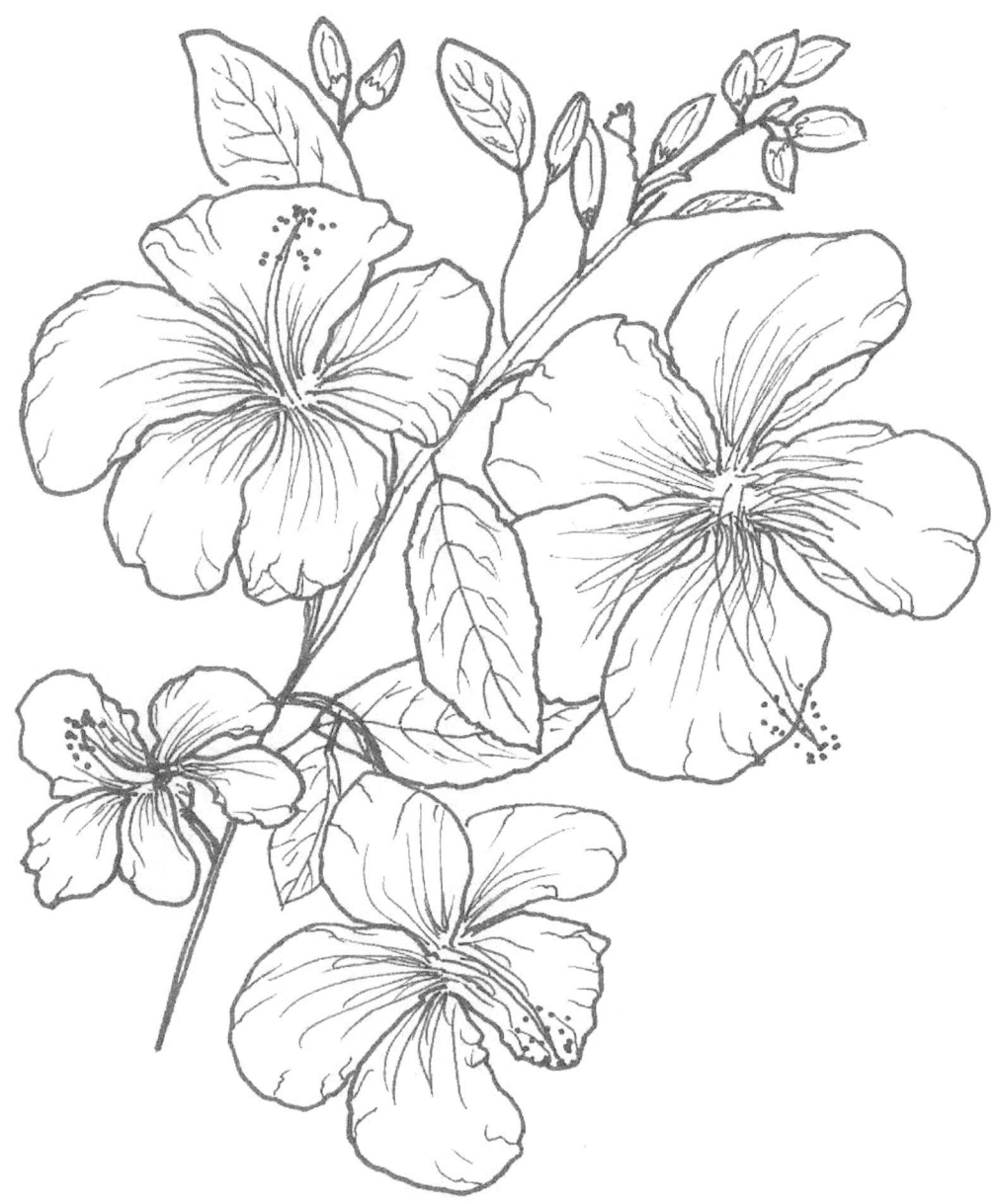

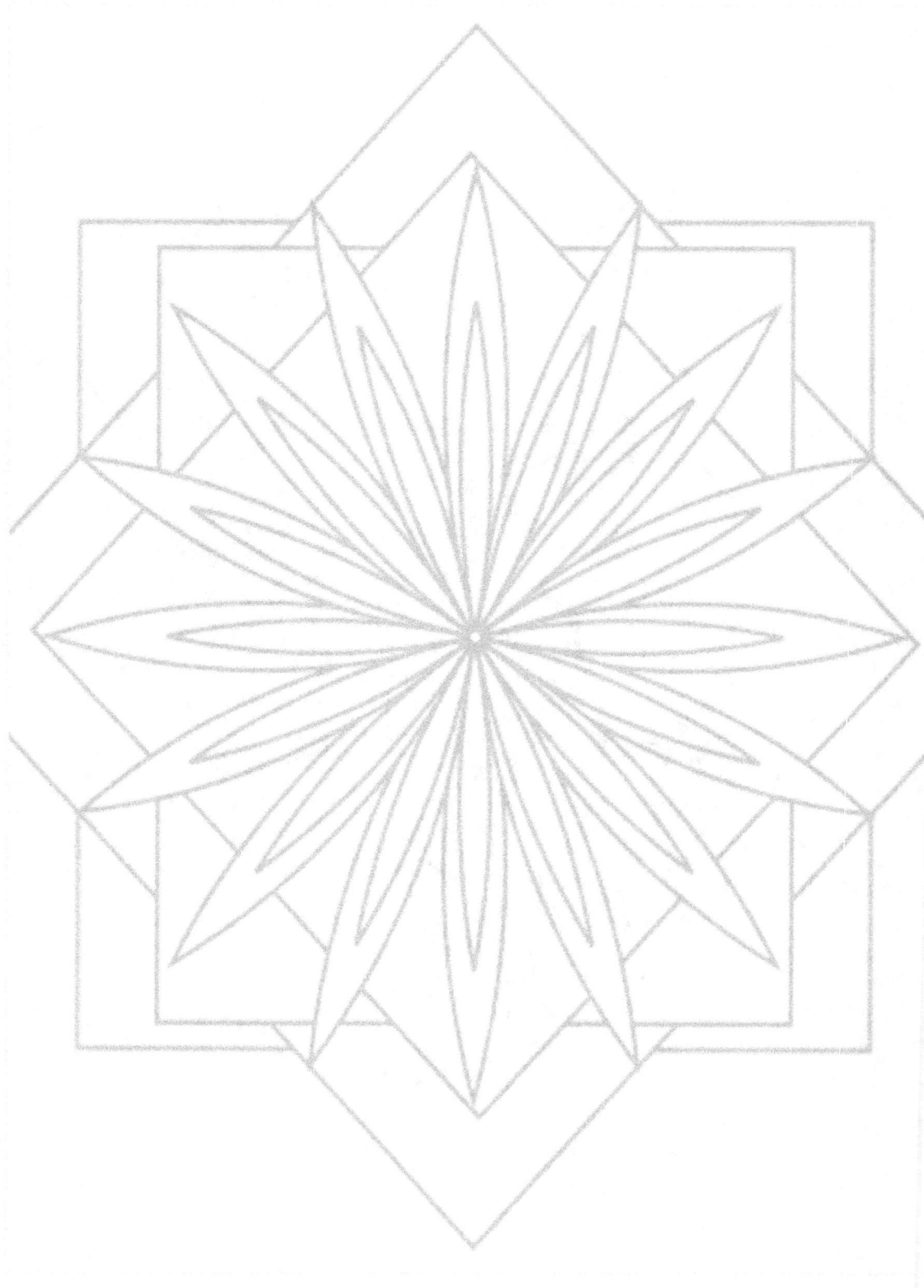

Copyrighted Material

Hibiscus

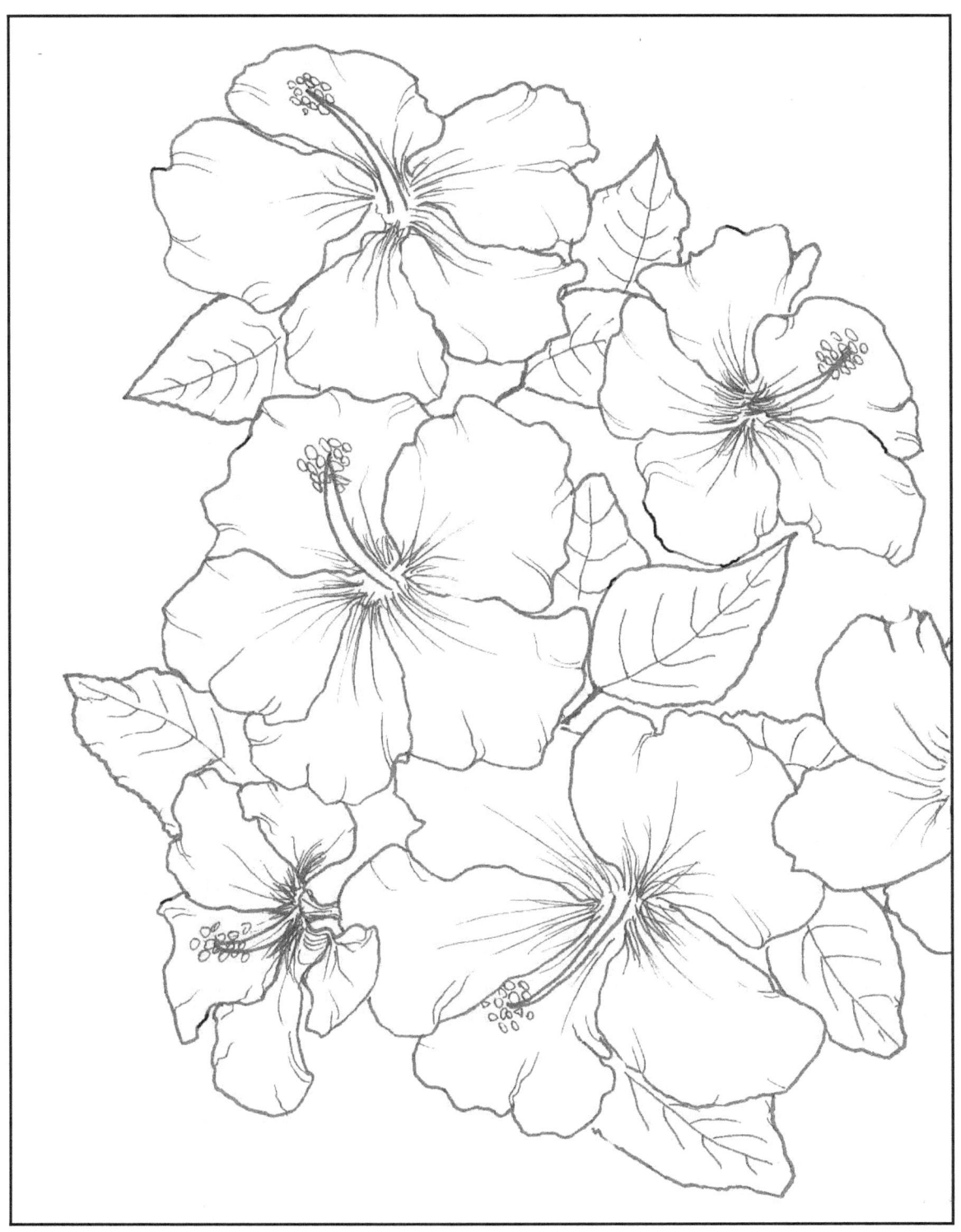

KD Coloring Studio

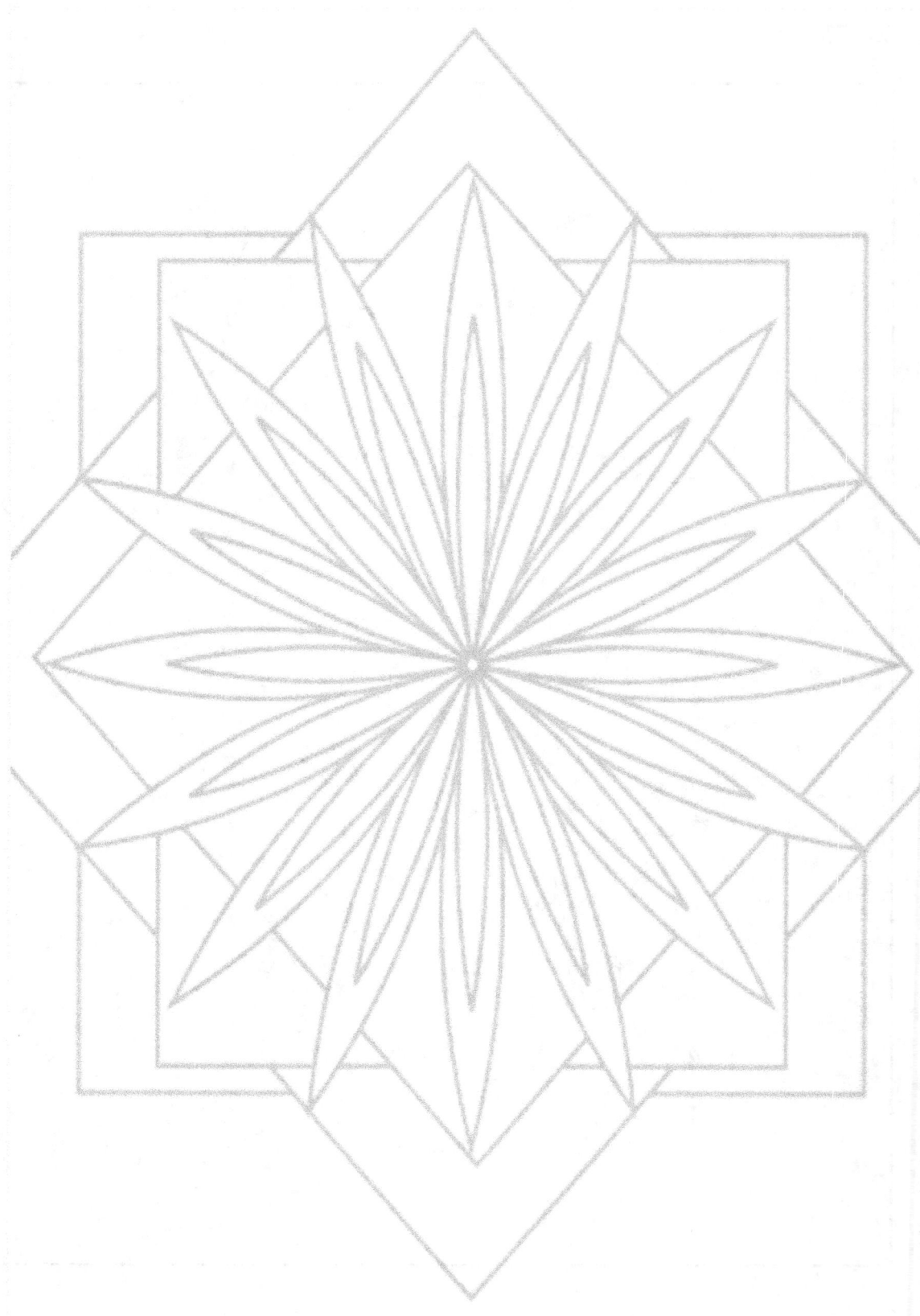

Copyrighted Material

Poppy

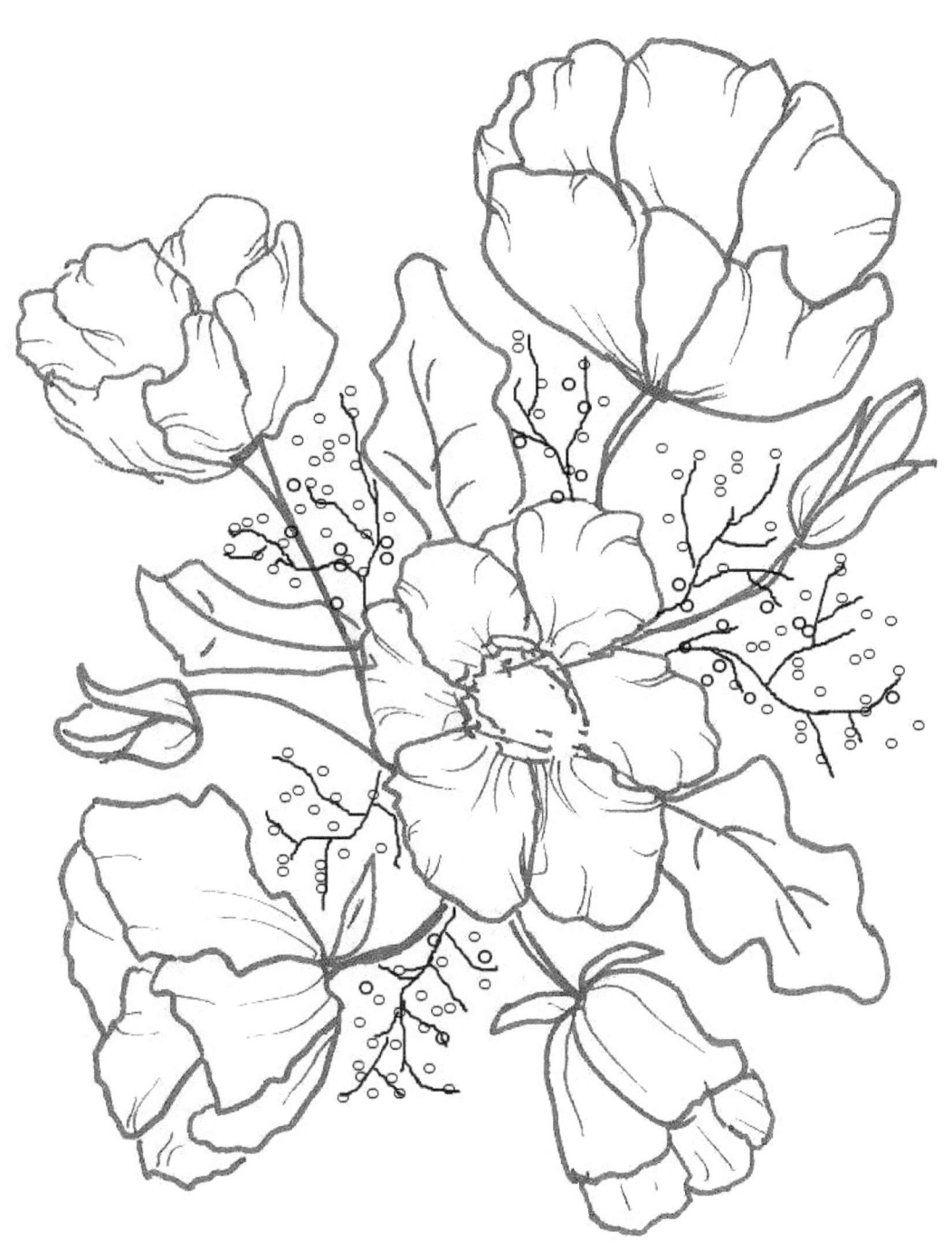

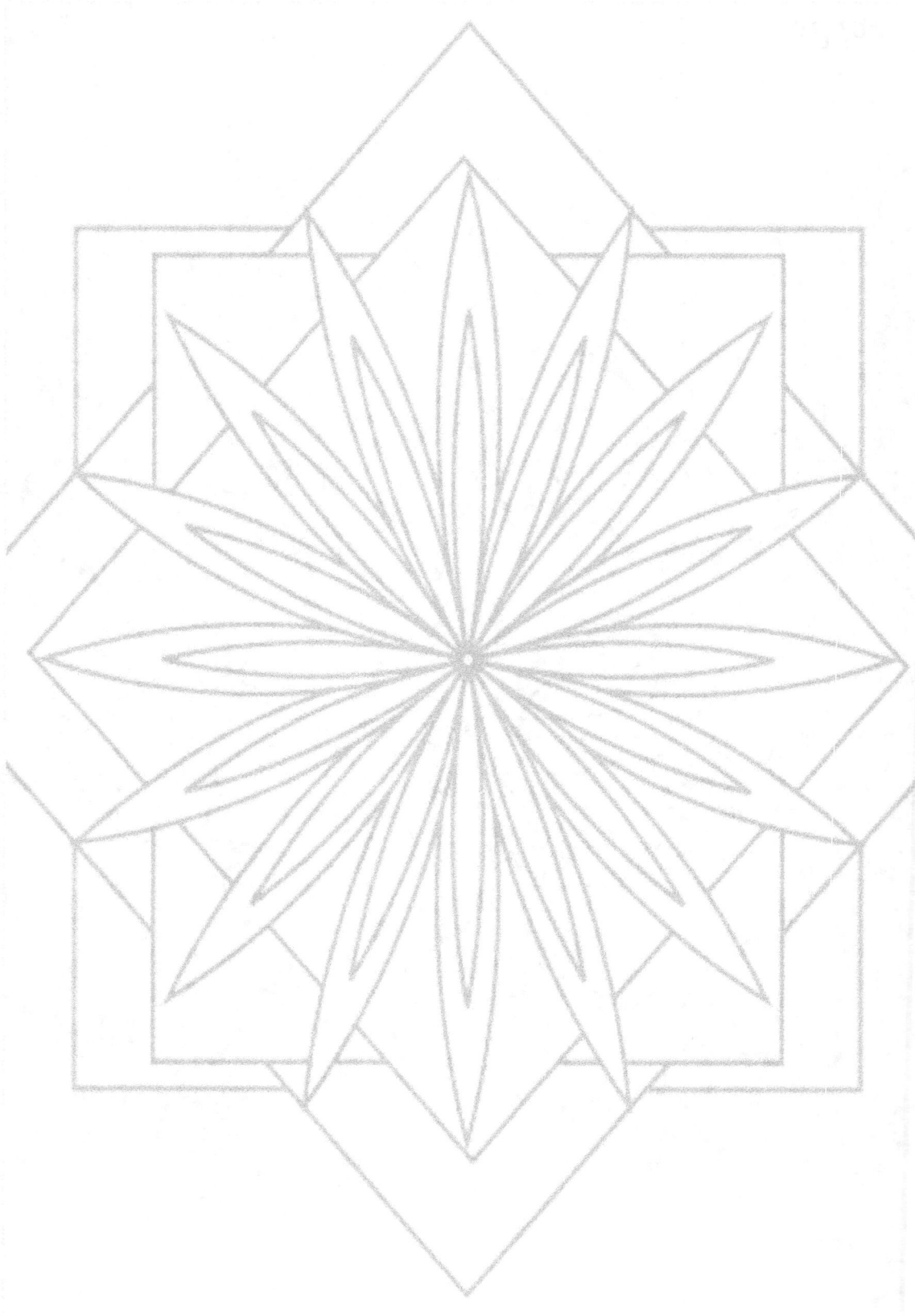

Copyrighted Material

Poppy

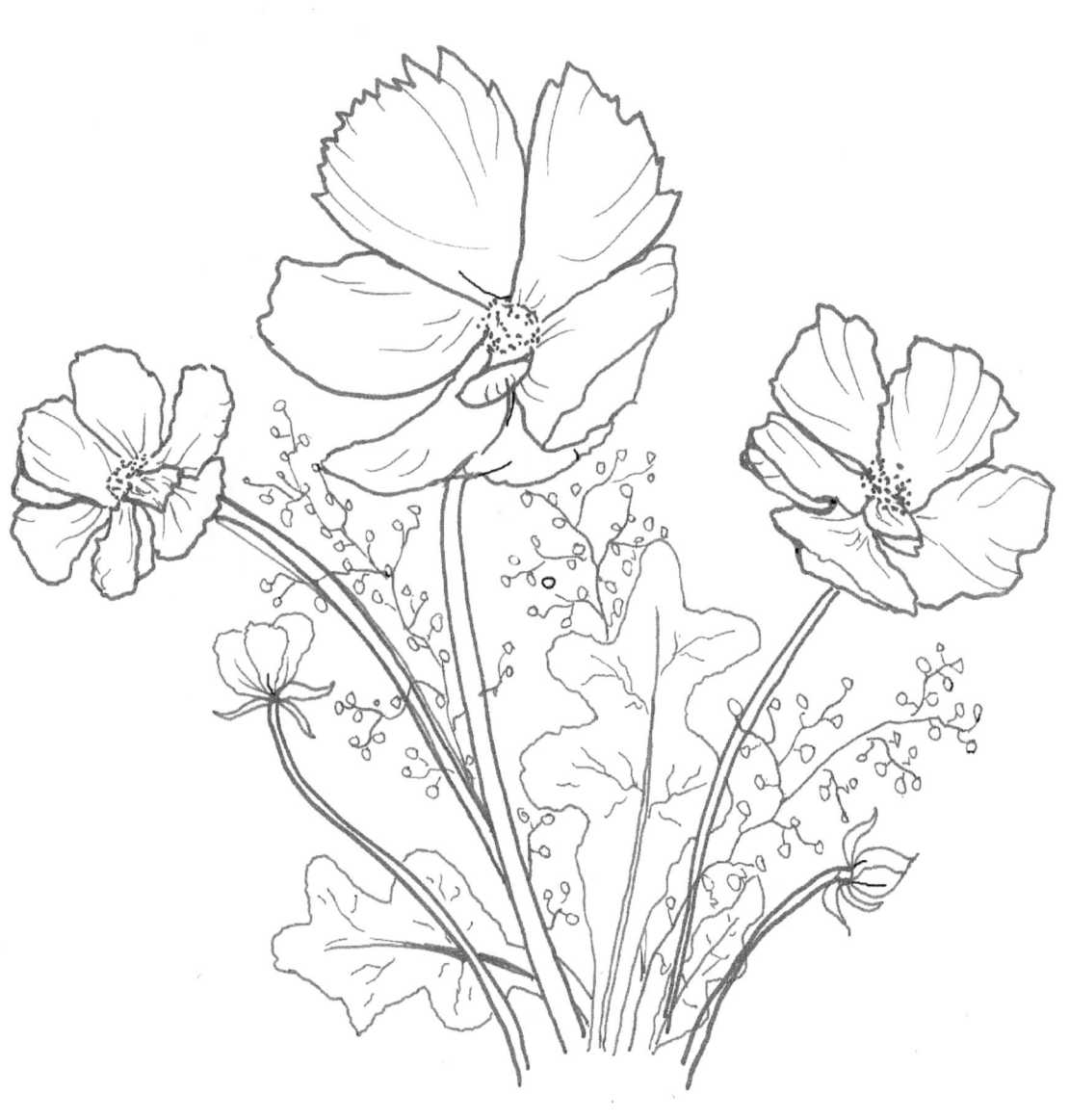

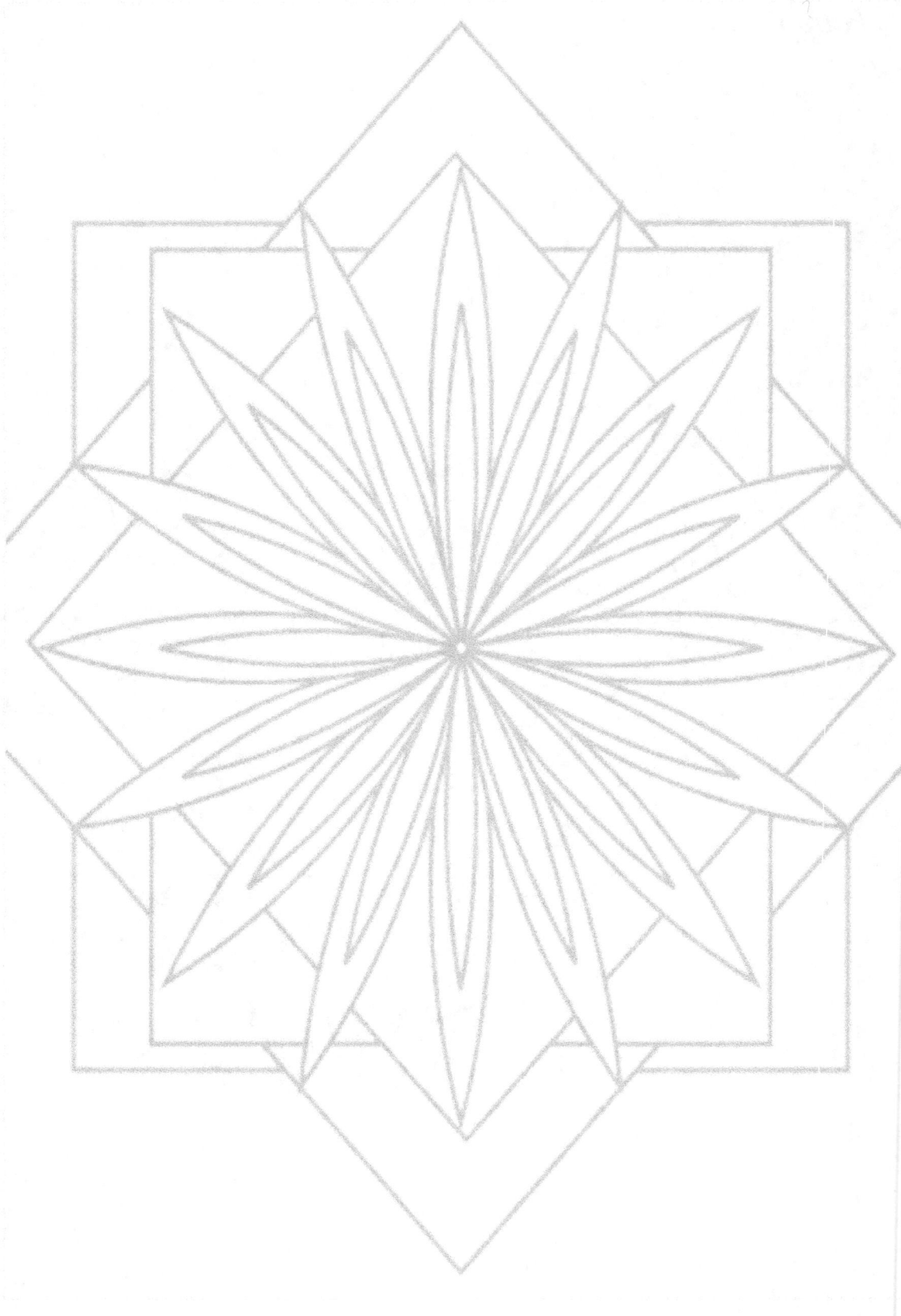

Copyrighted Material

Chrysanthemum

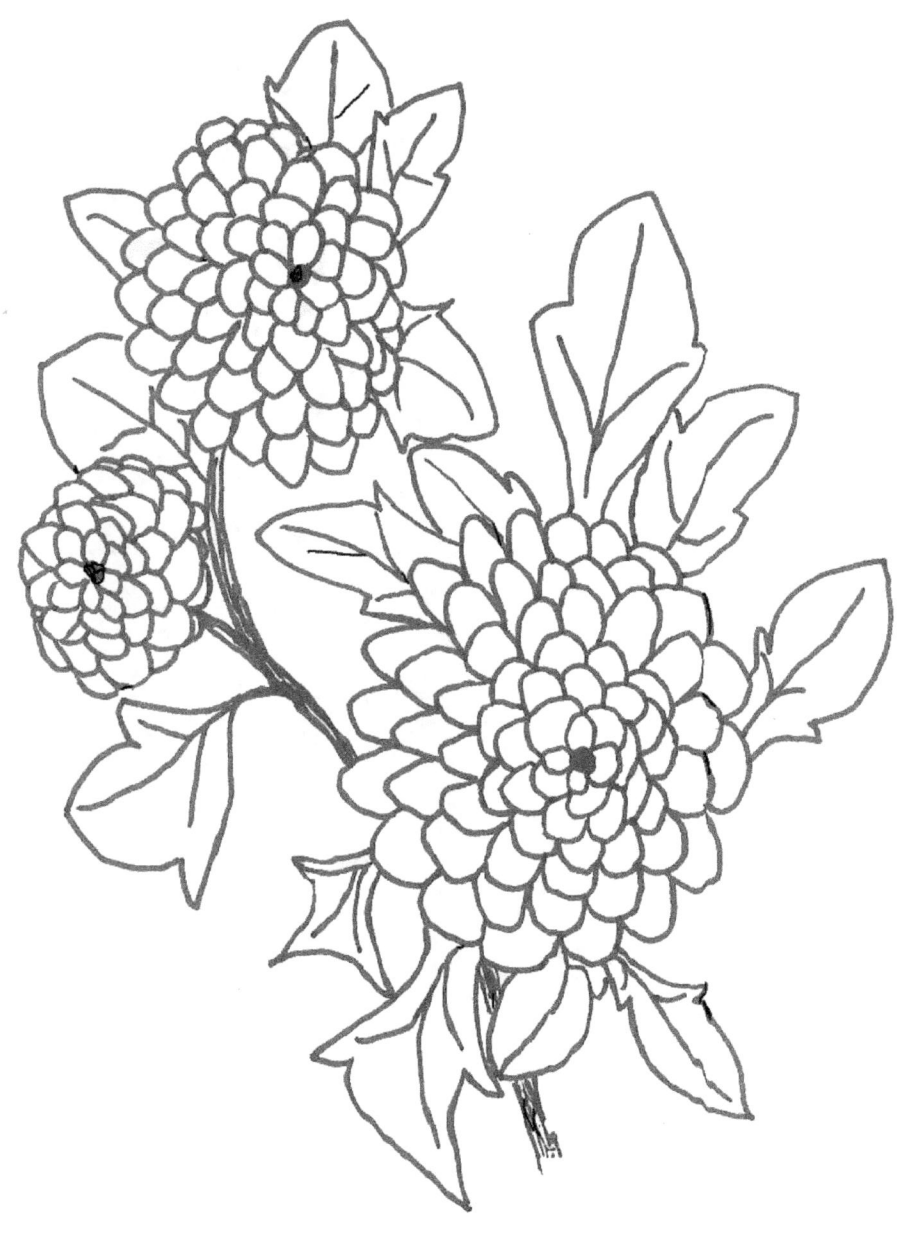

KD Coloring Studio

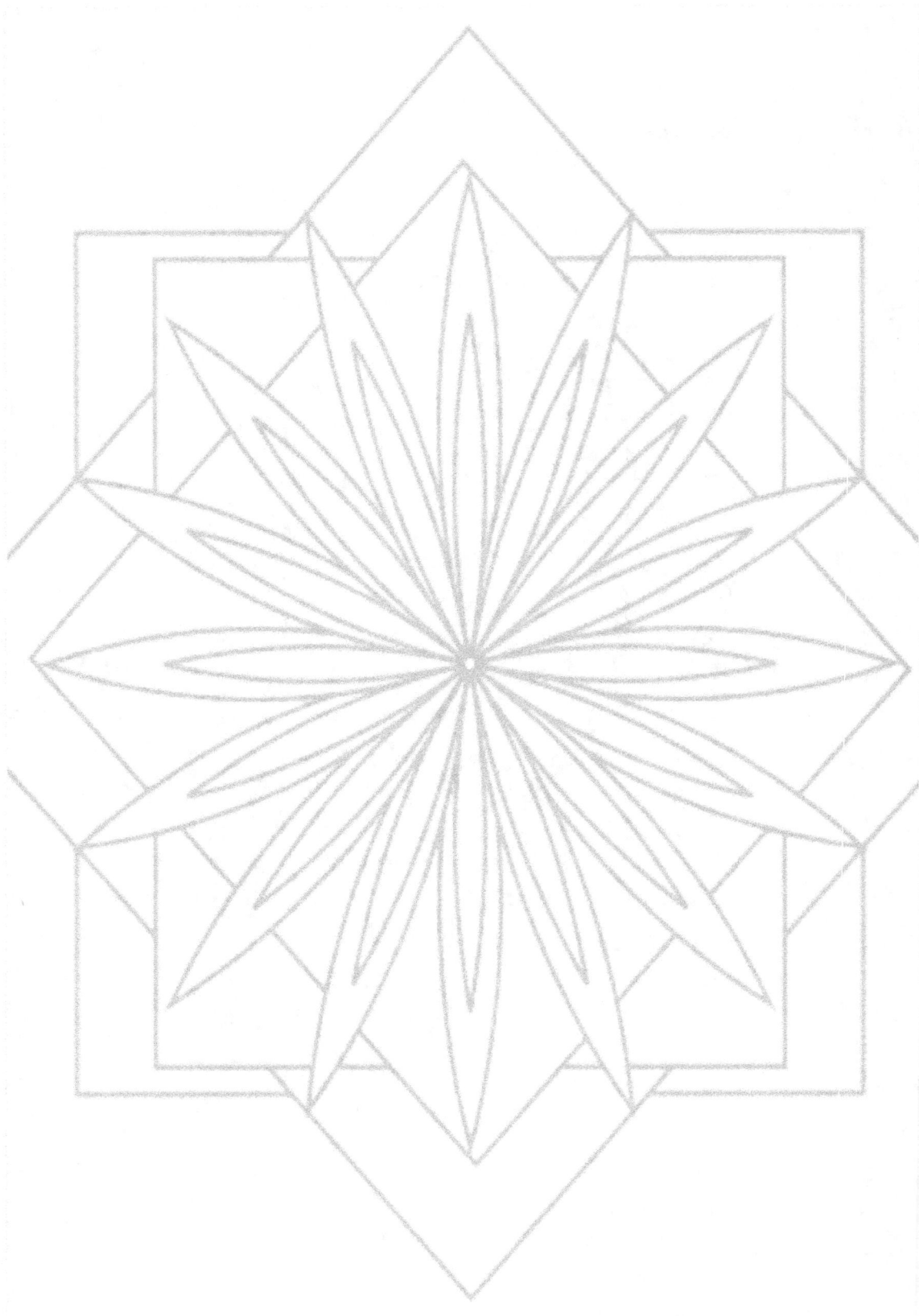

Copyrighted Material

Ginger Flower

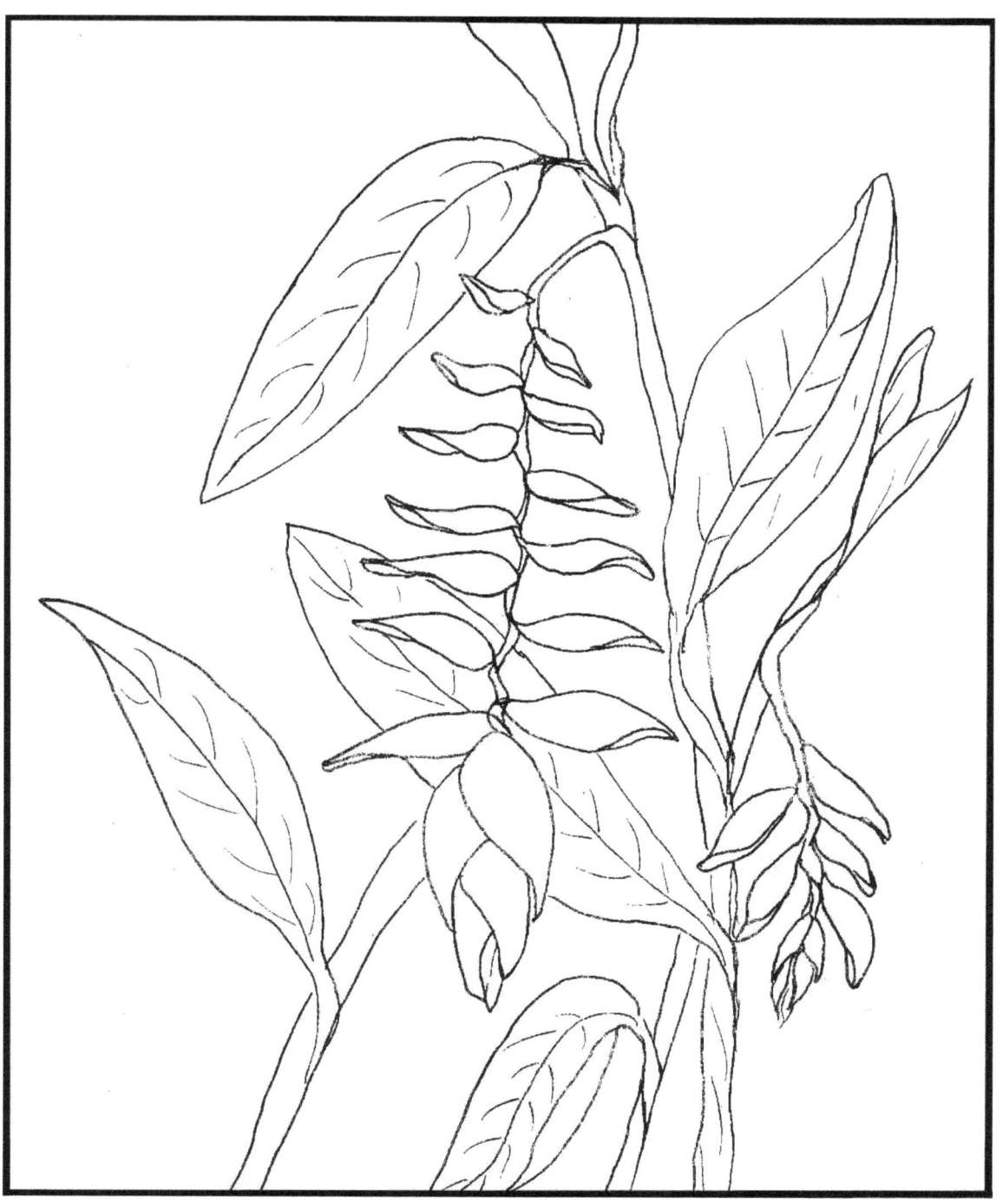

KD Coloring Studio

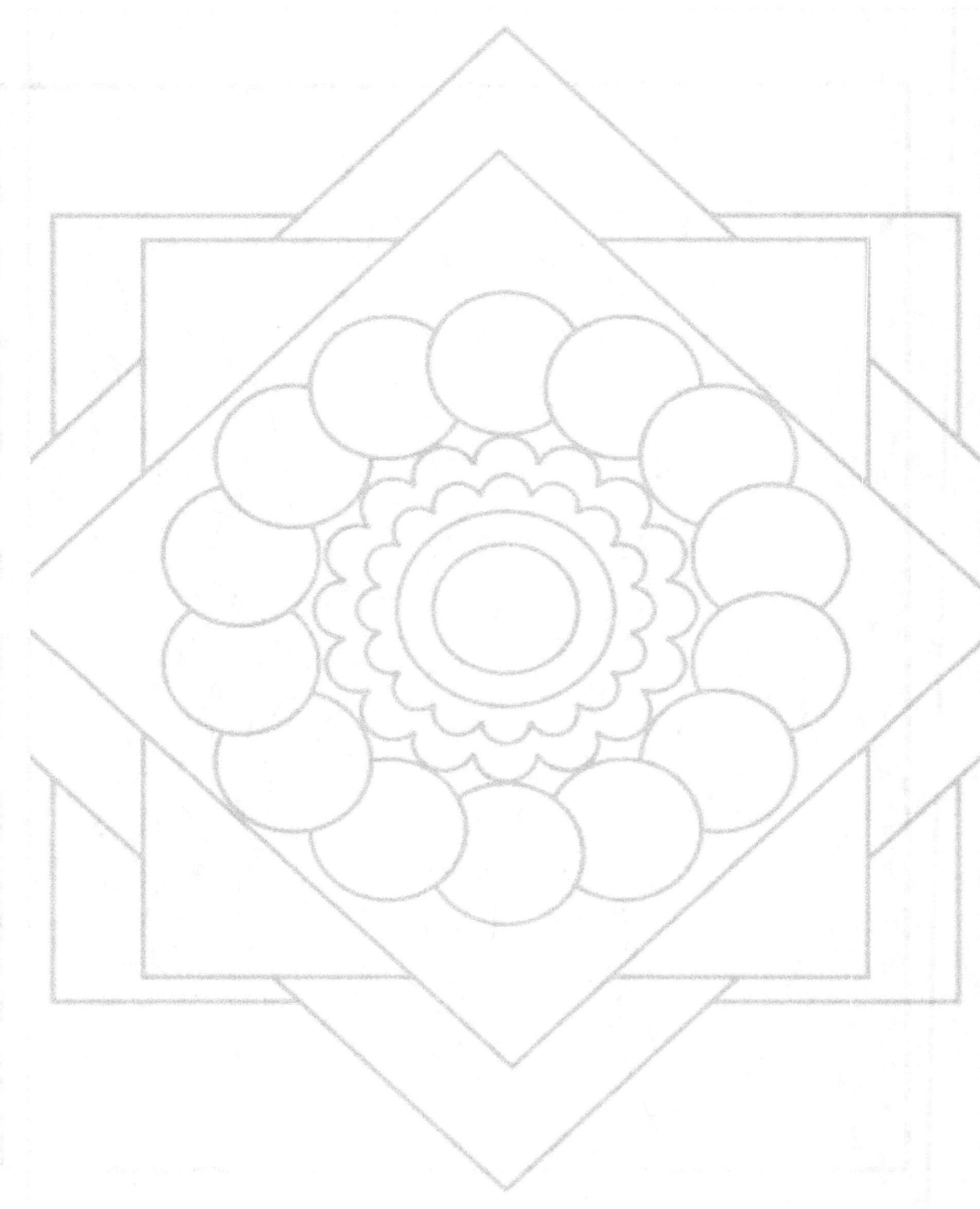

Copyrighted Material

Peony

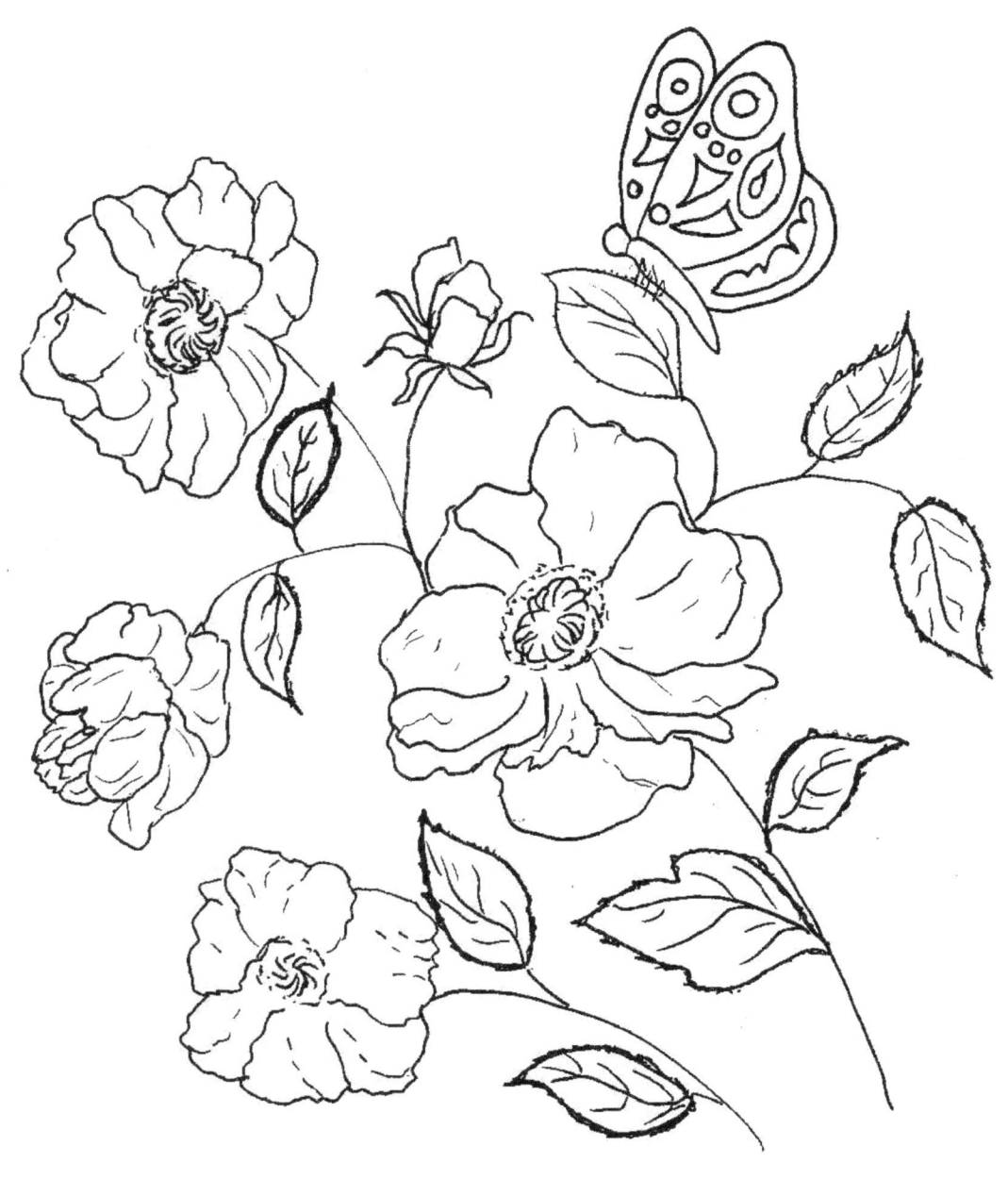

KD Coloring Studio

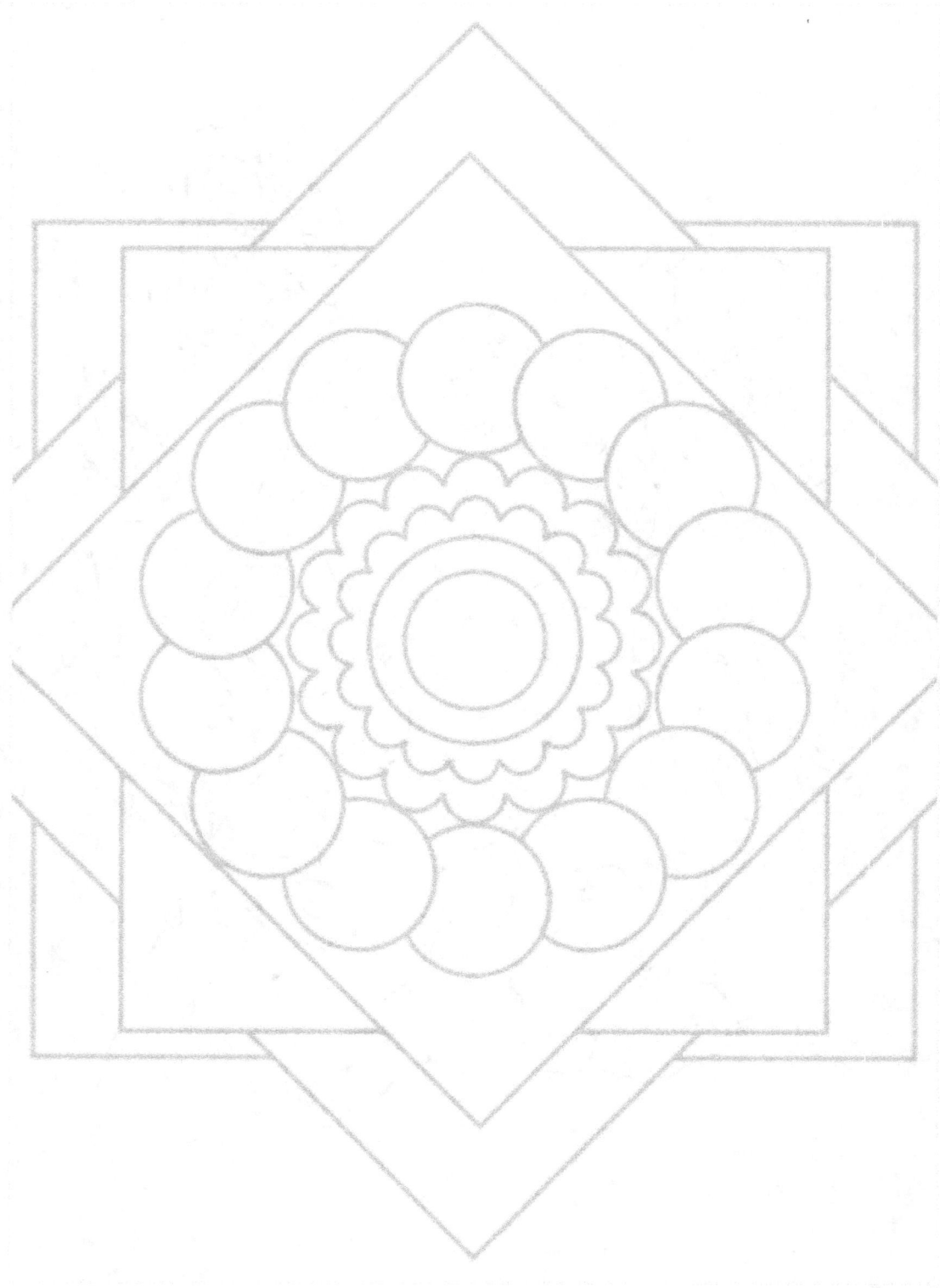

Copyrighted Material

Anthurium

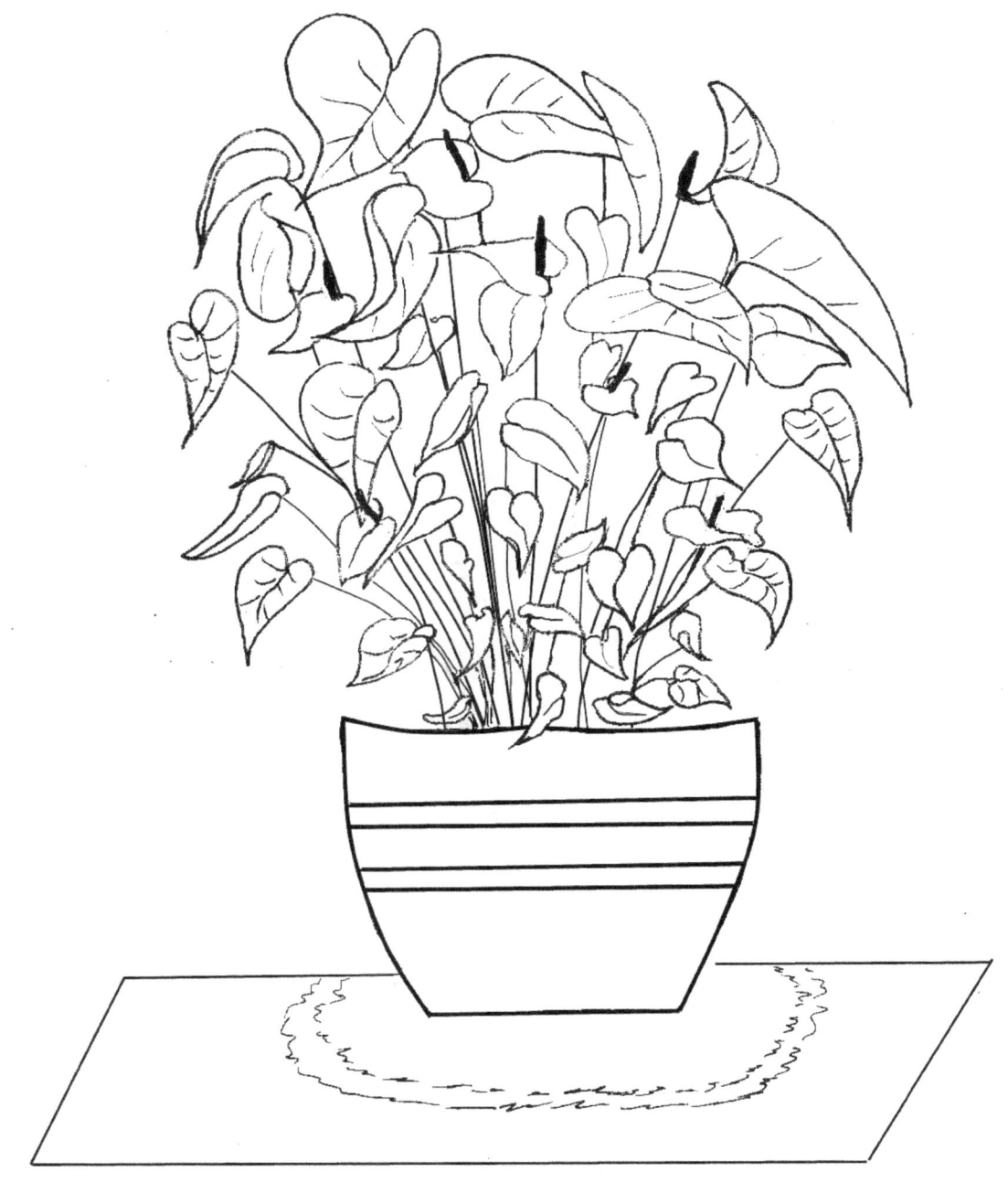

KD Coloring Studio

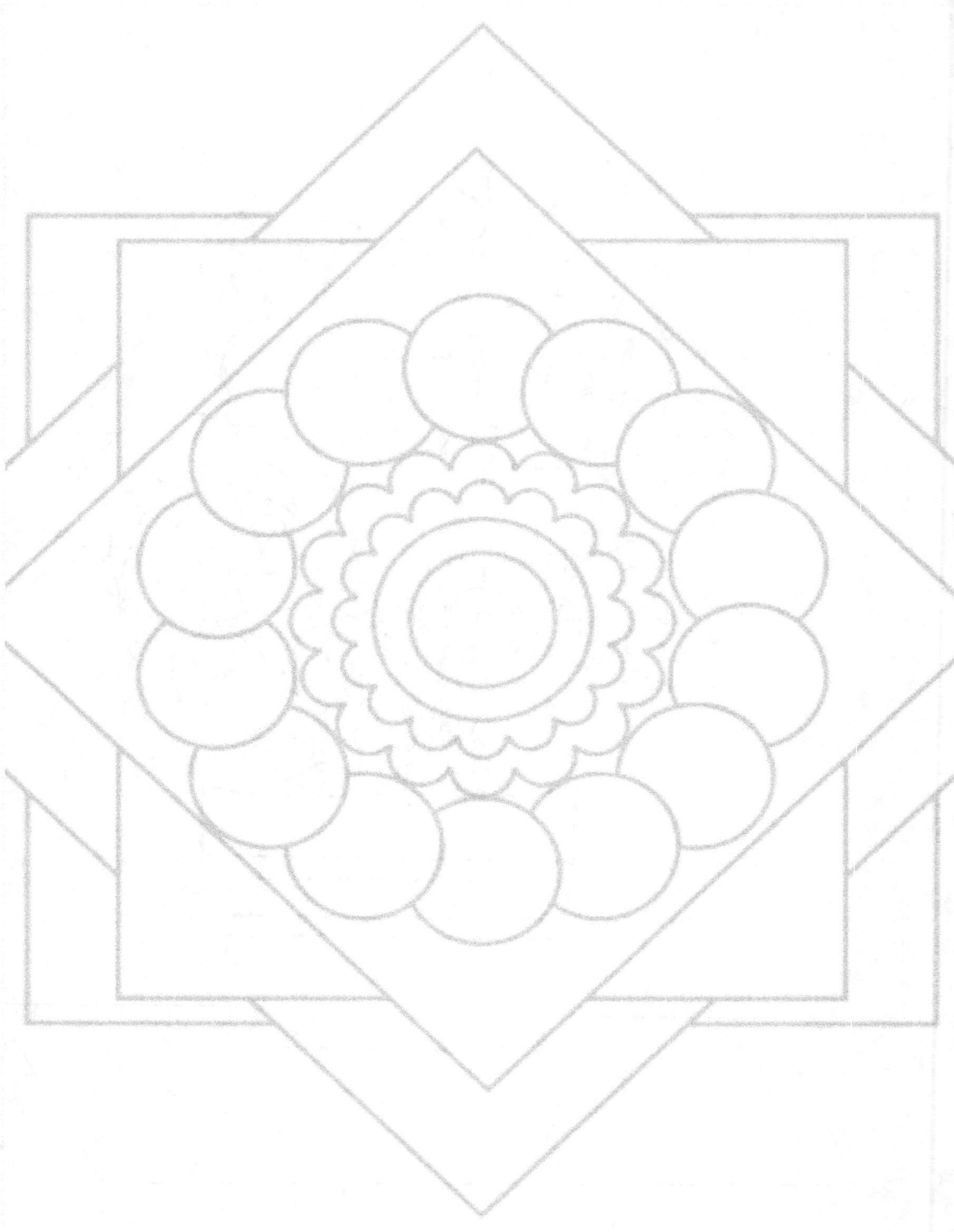

Copyrighted Material

Peony

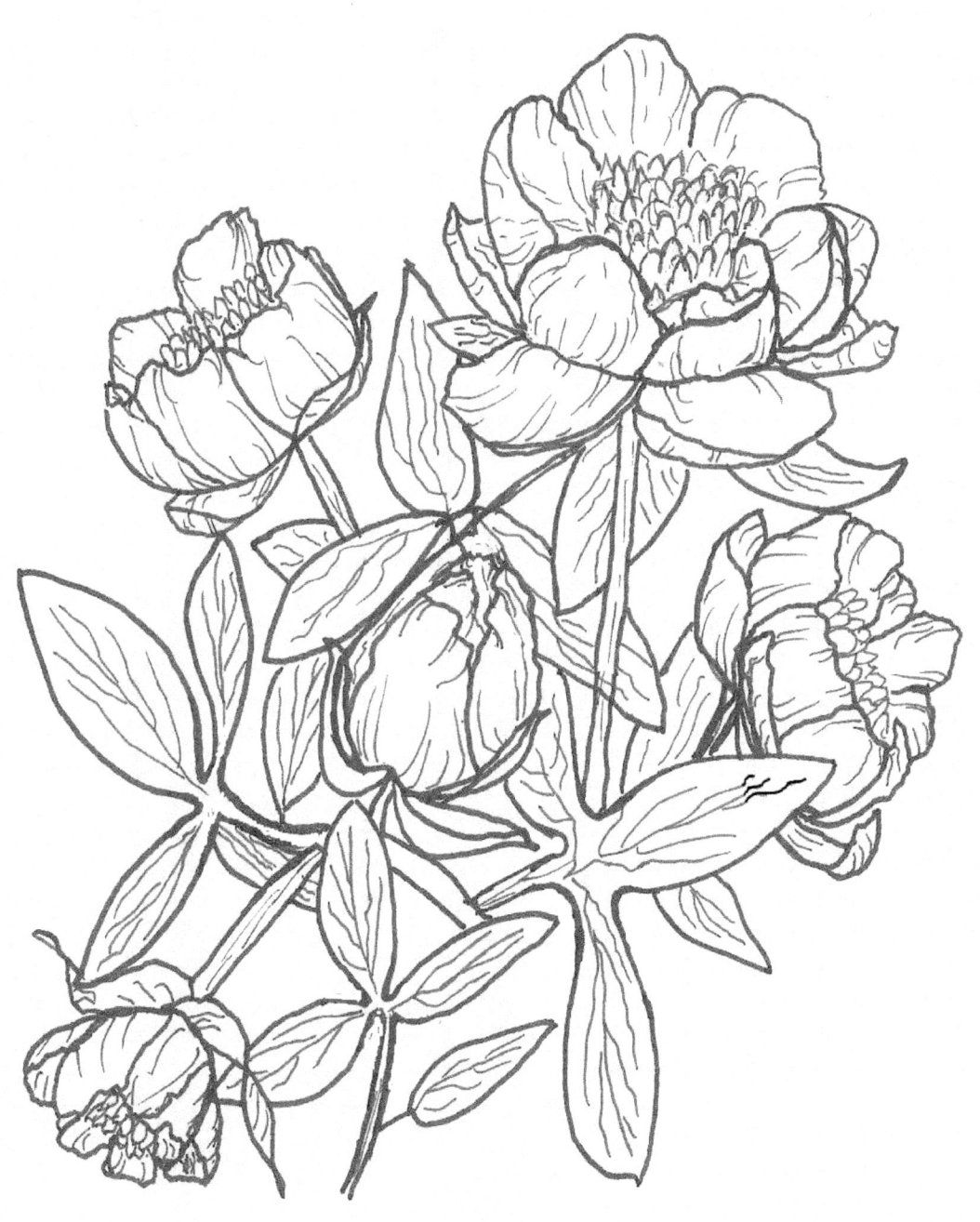

KD Coloring Studio

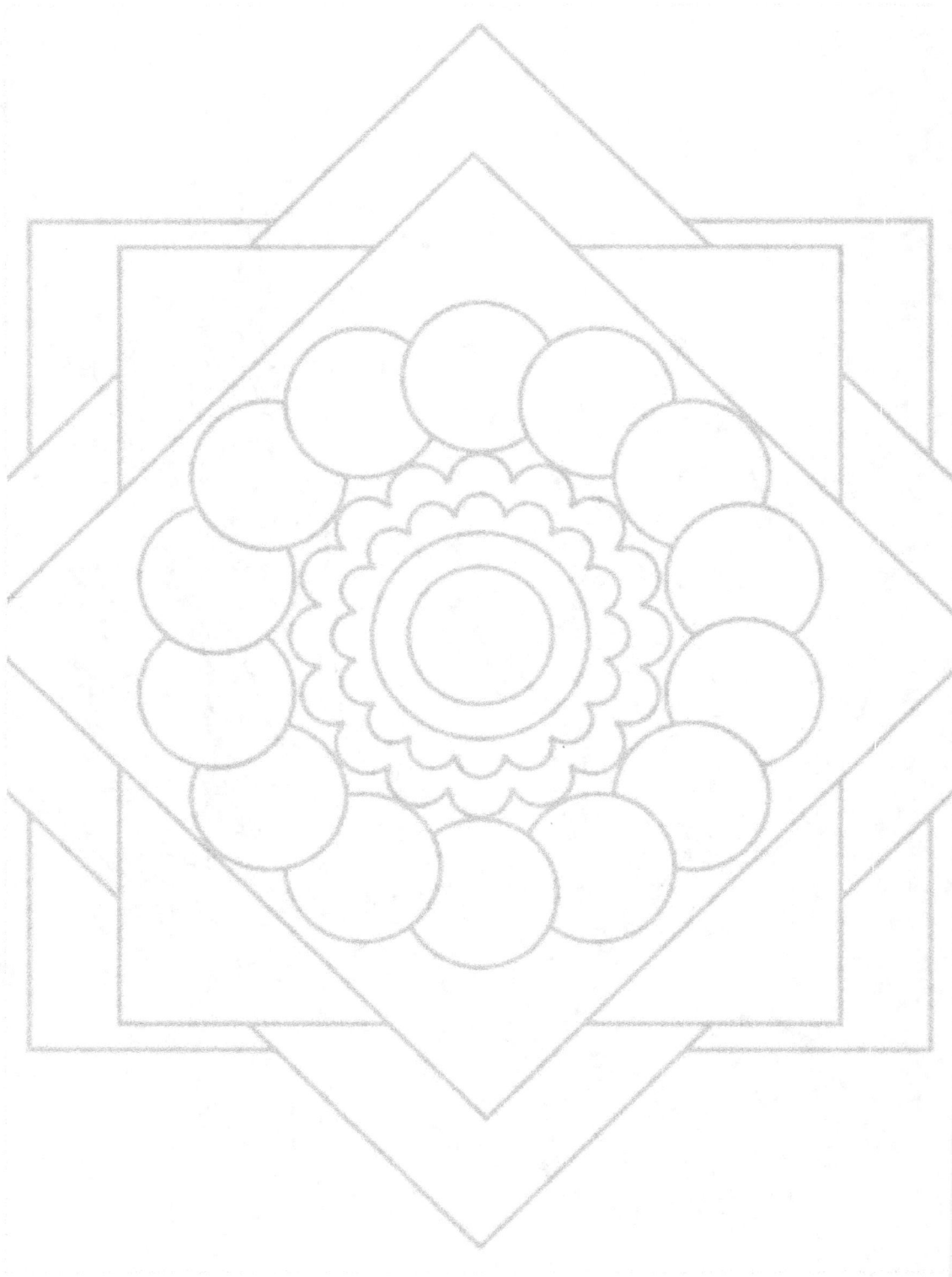

Copyrighted Material

Rose

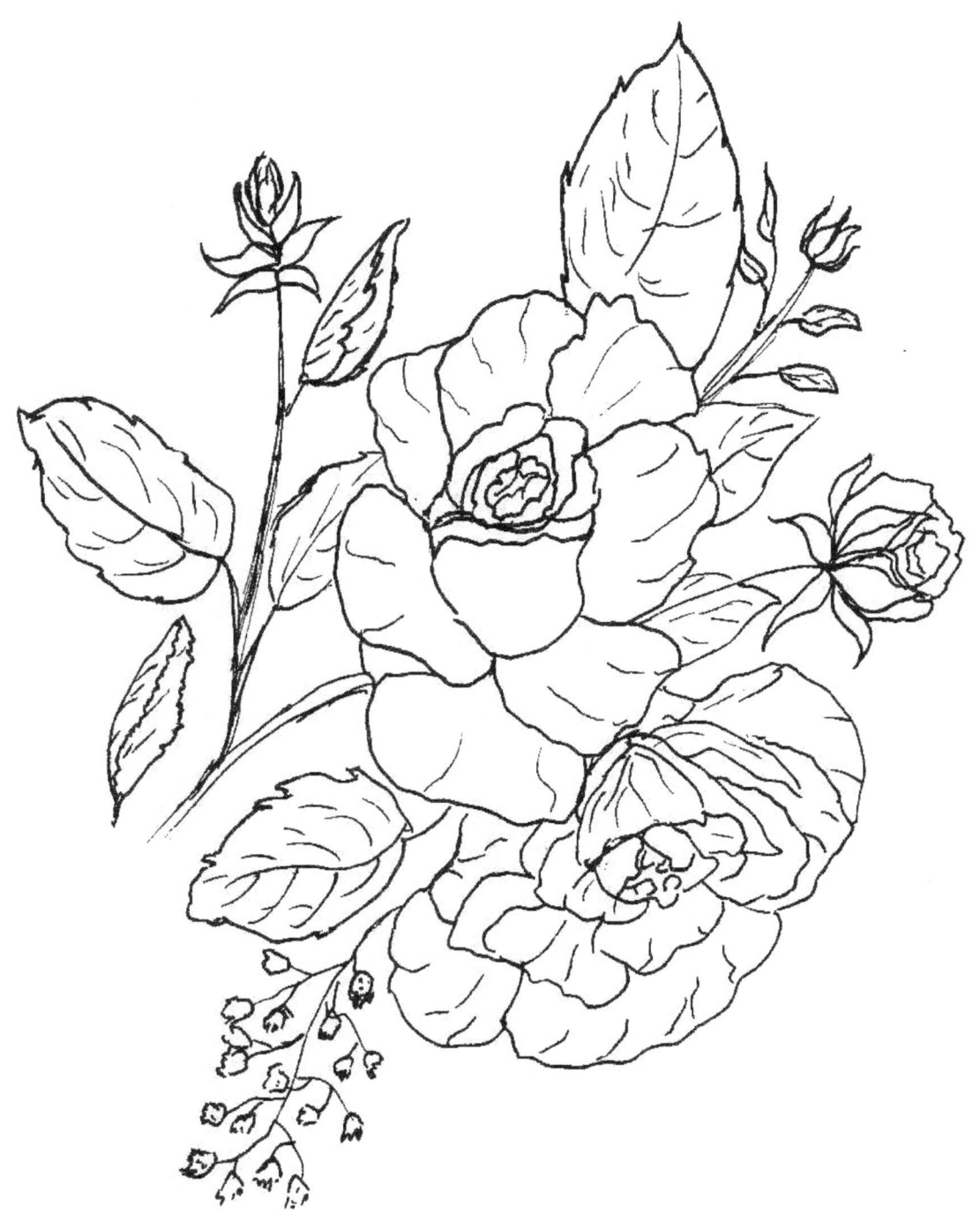

KD Coloring Studio

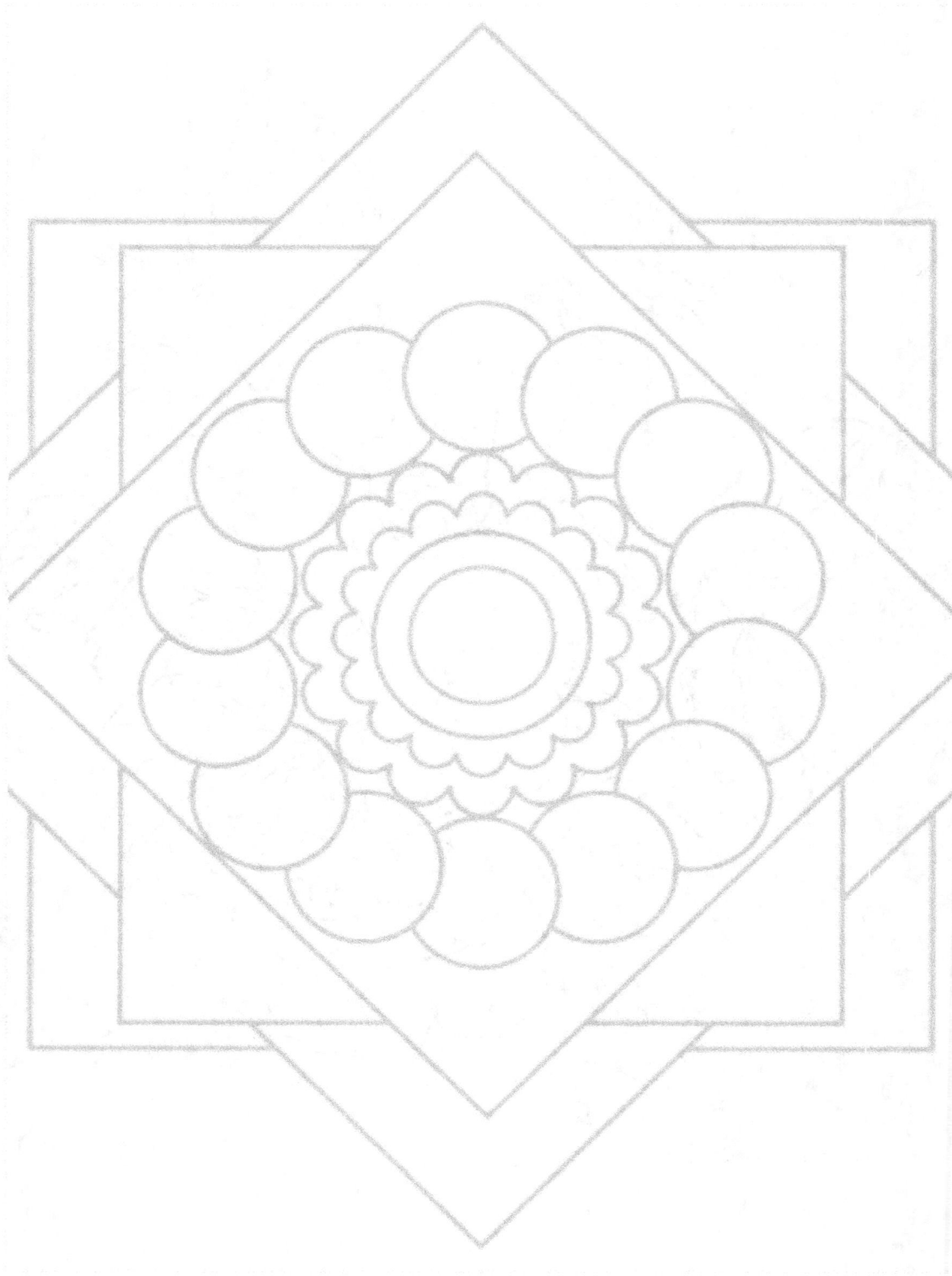

Copyrighted Material

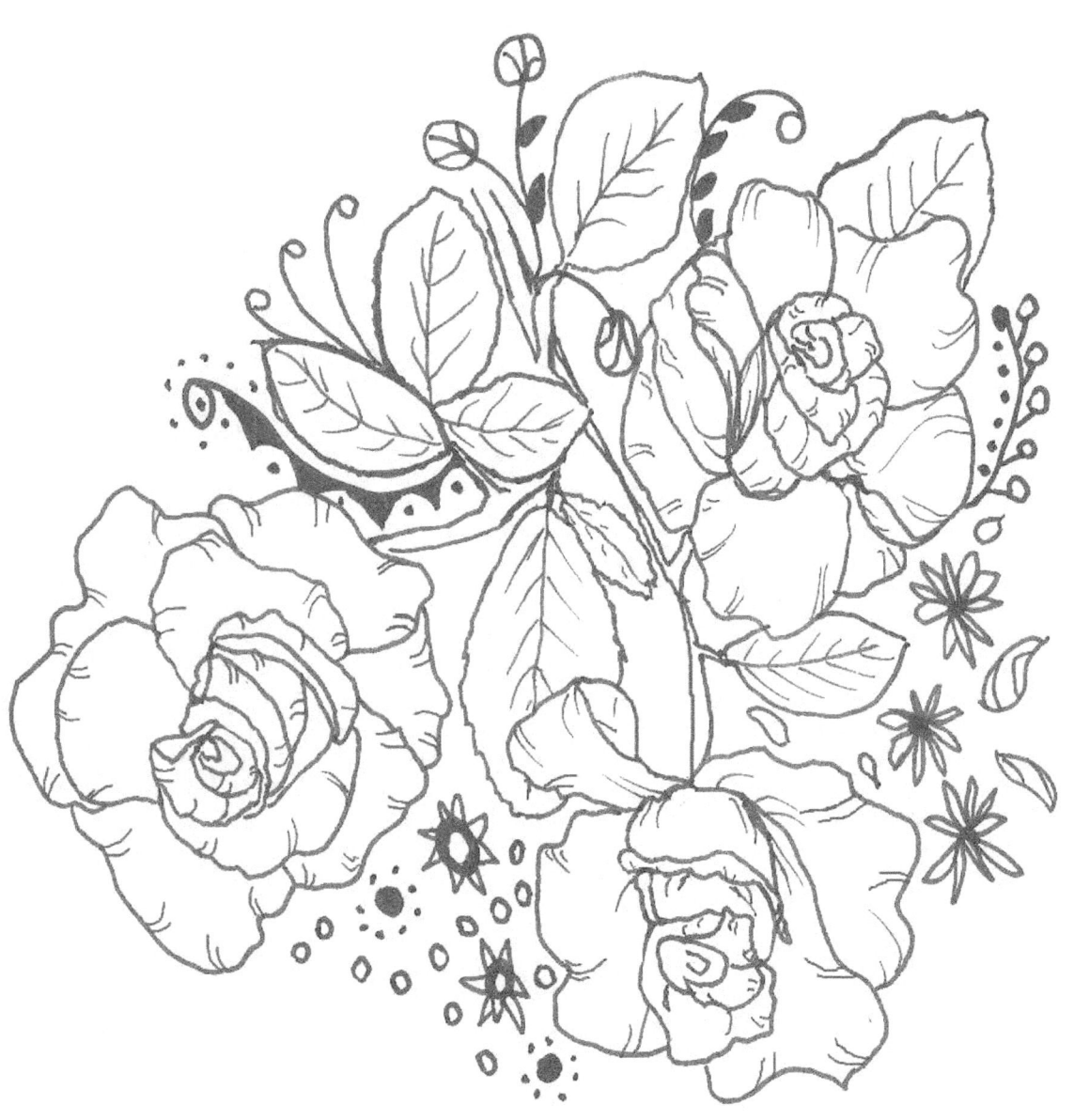

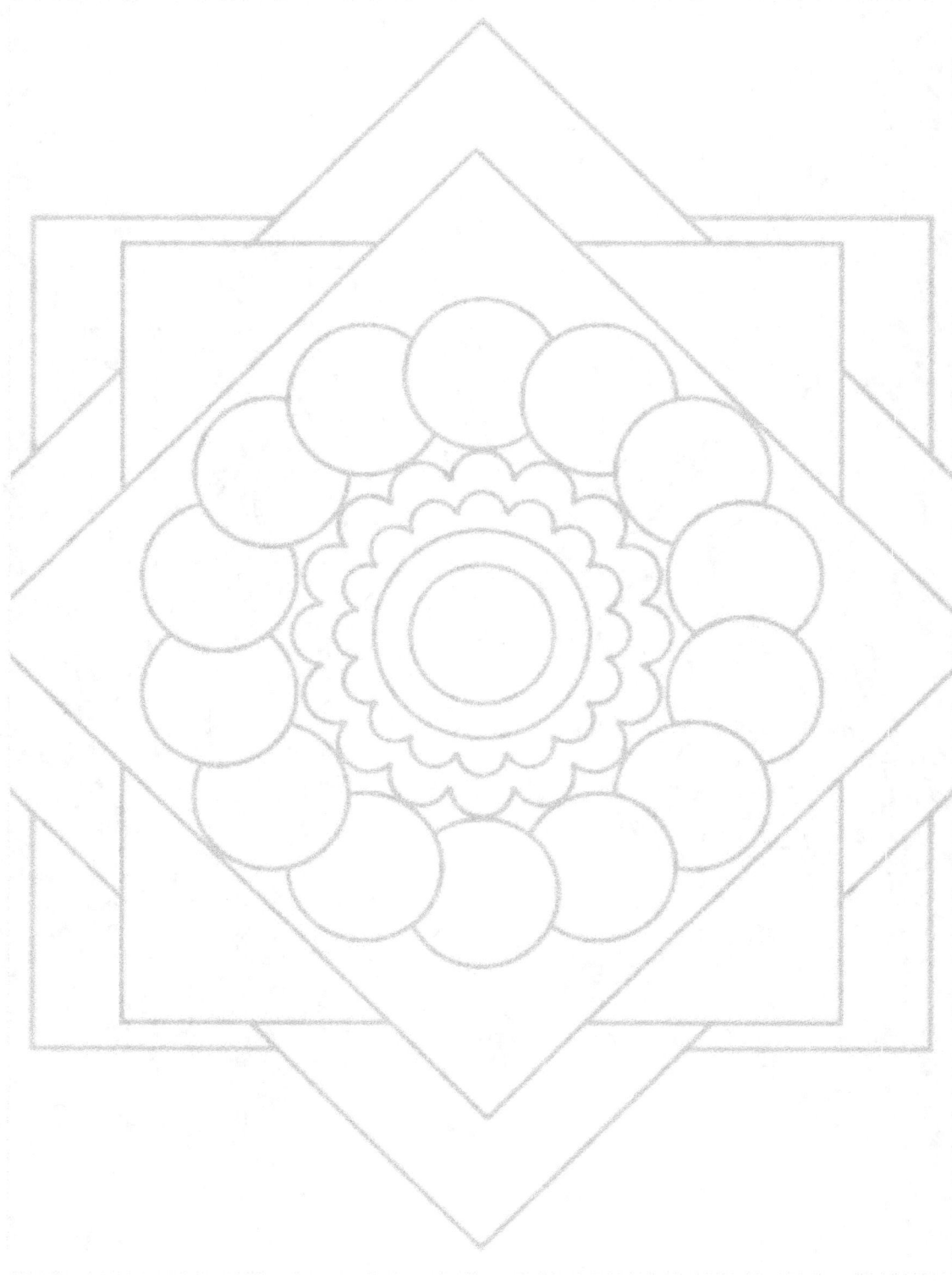

Copyrighted Material

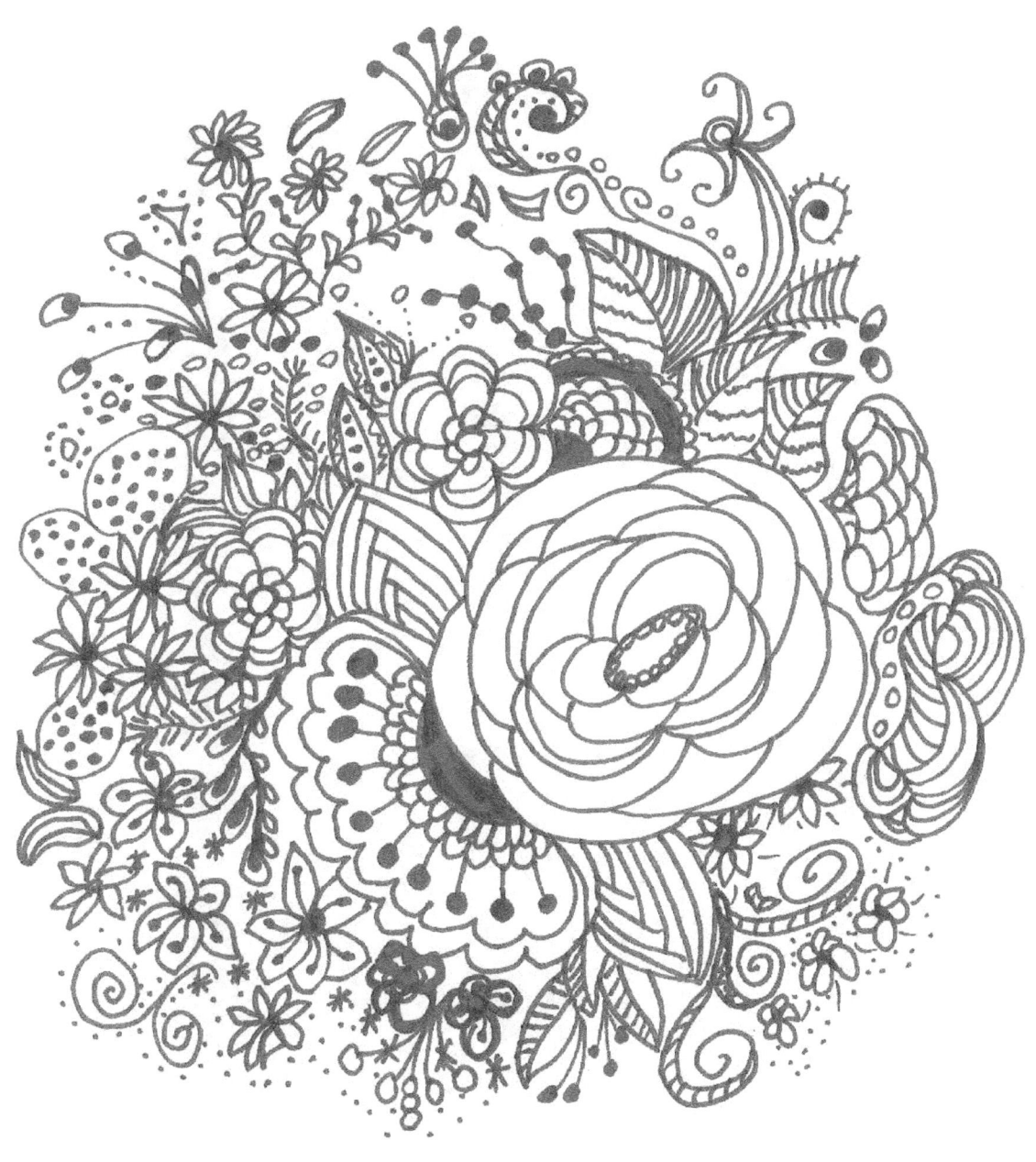

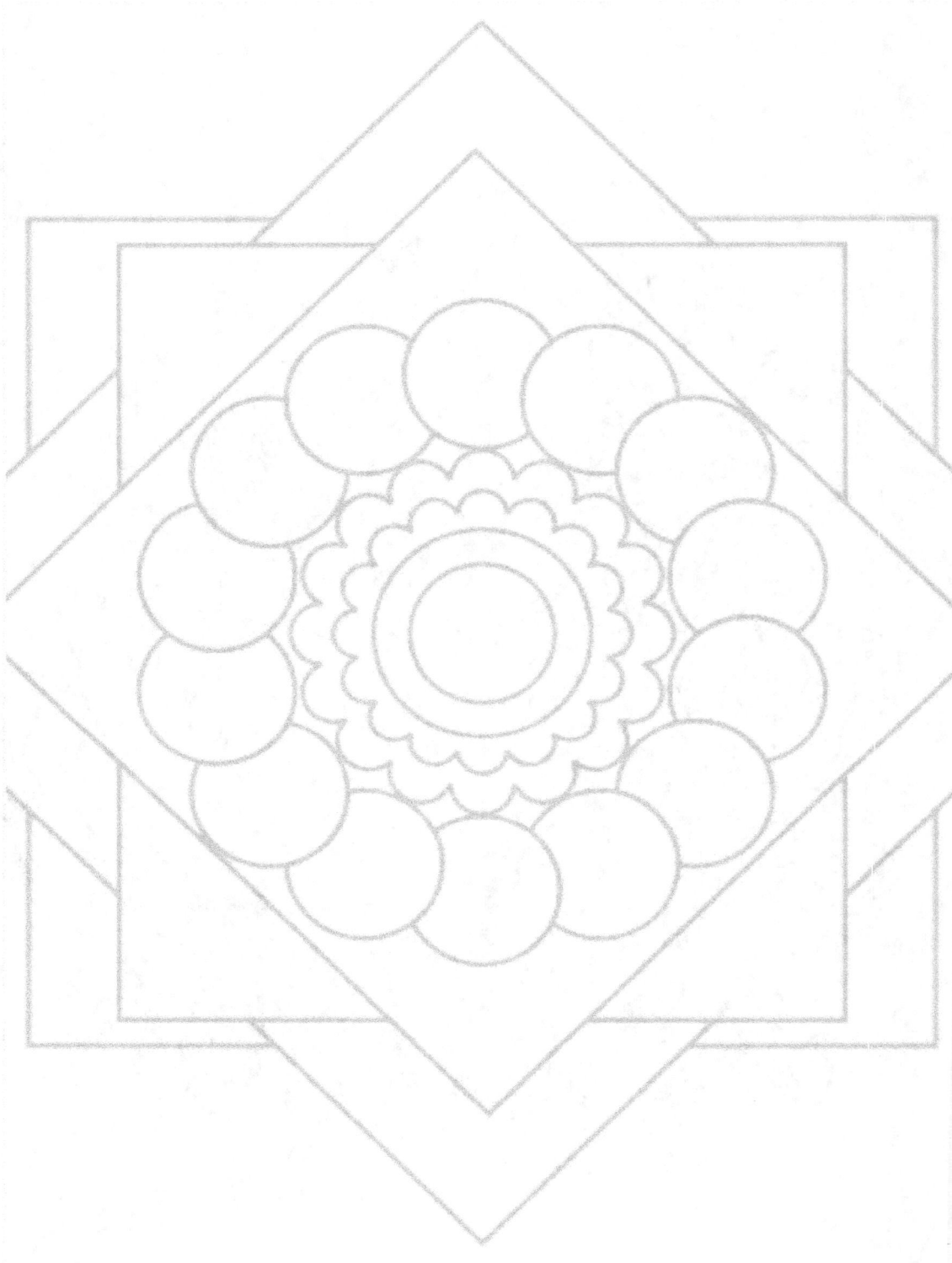

Copyrighted Material

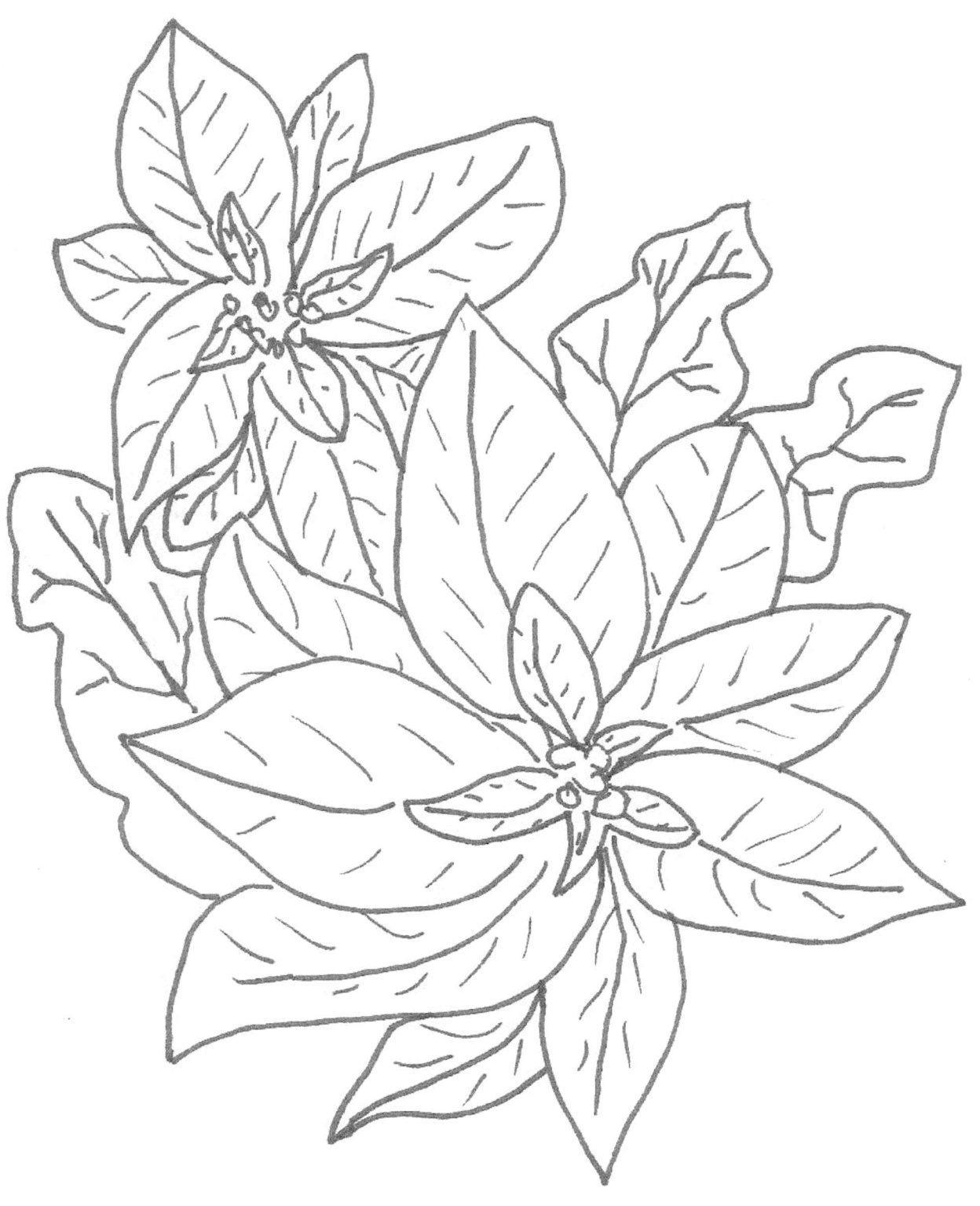

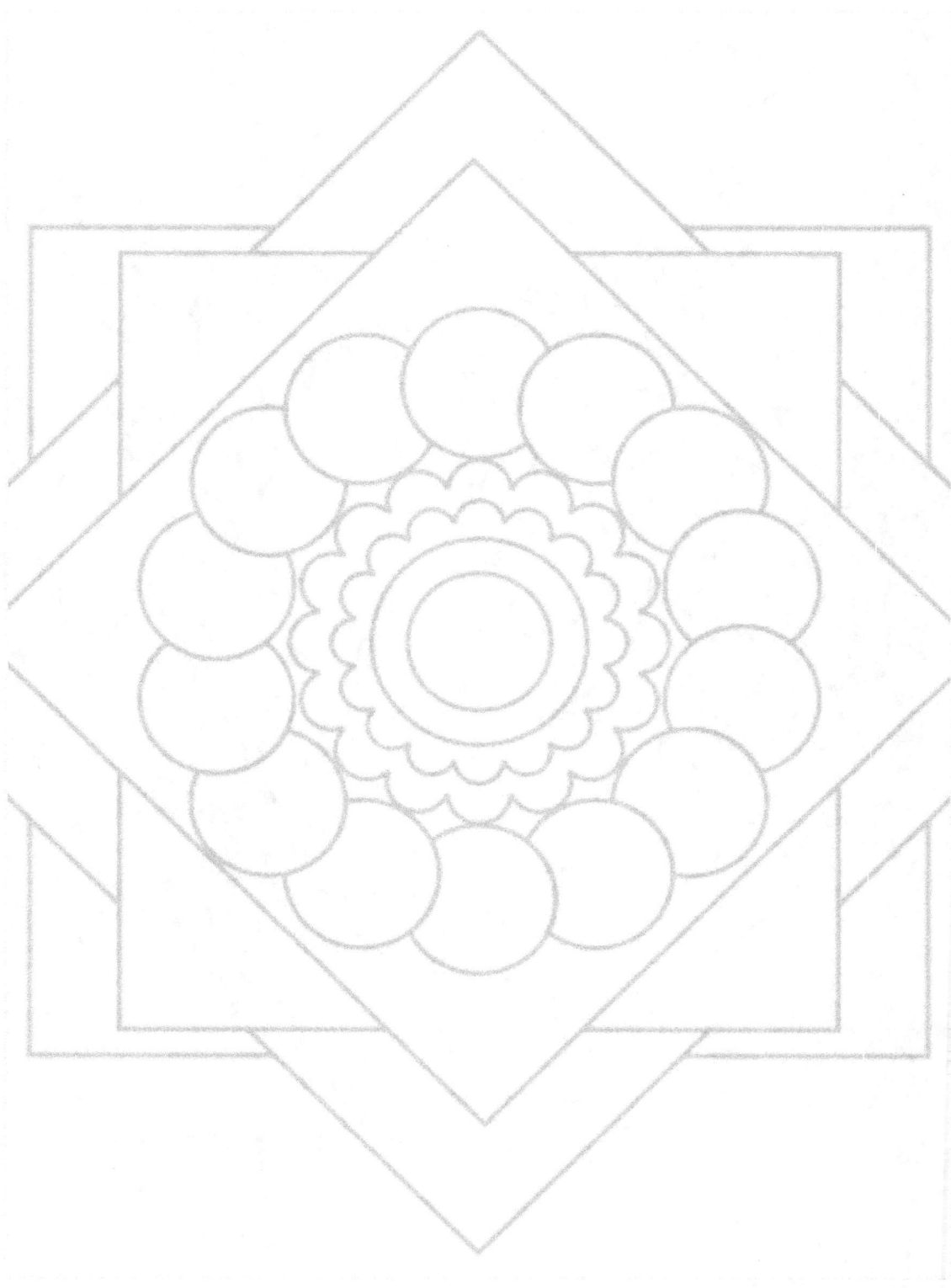

Copyrighted Material

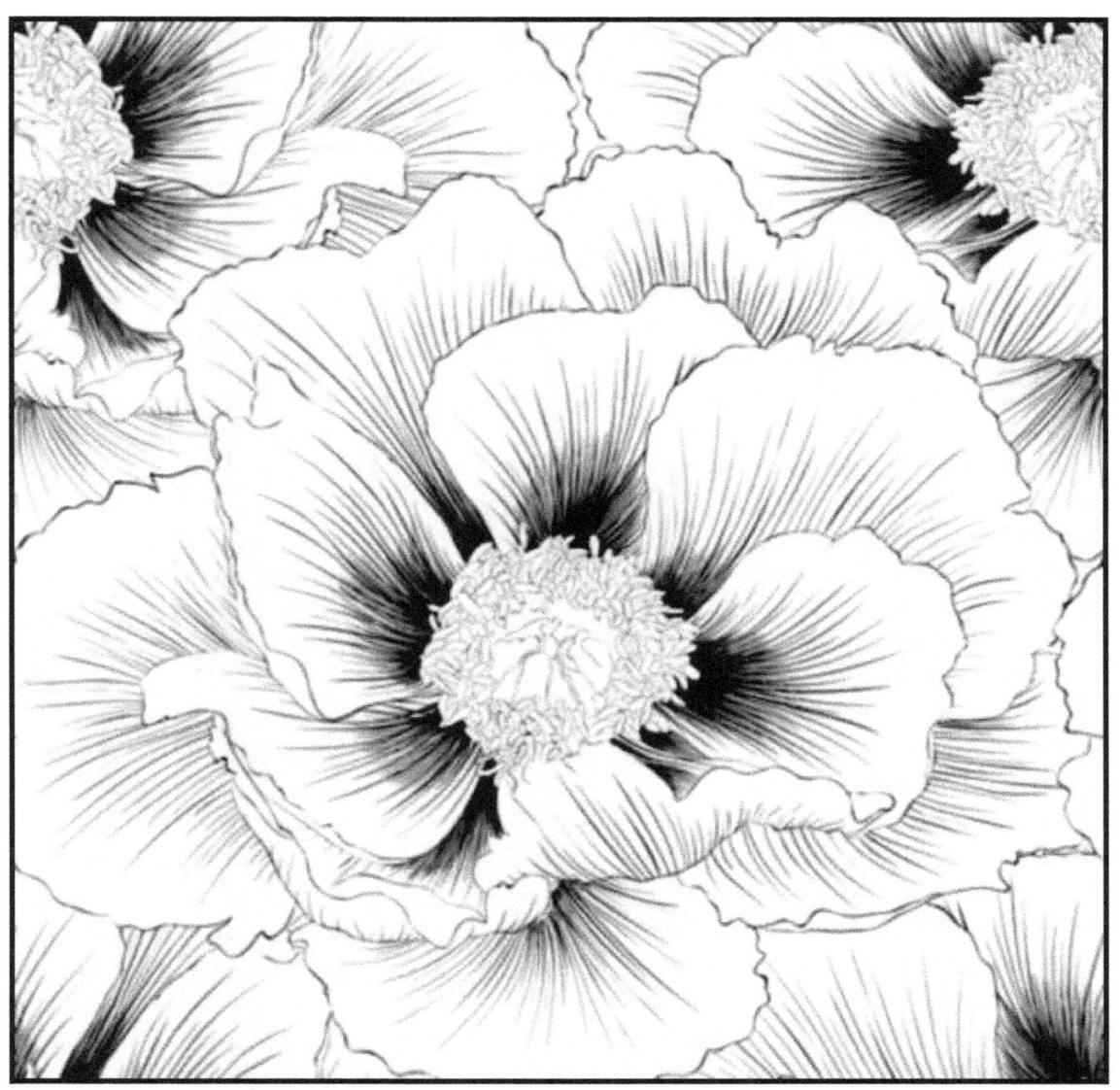

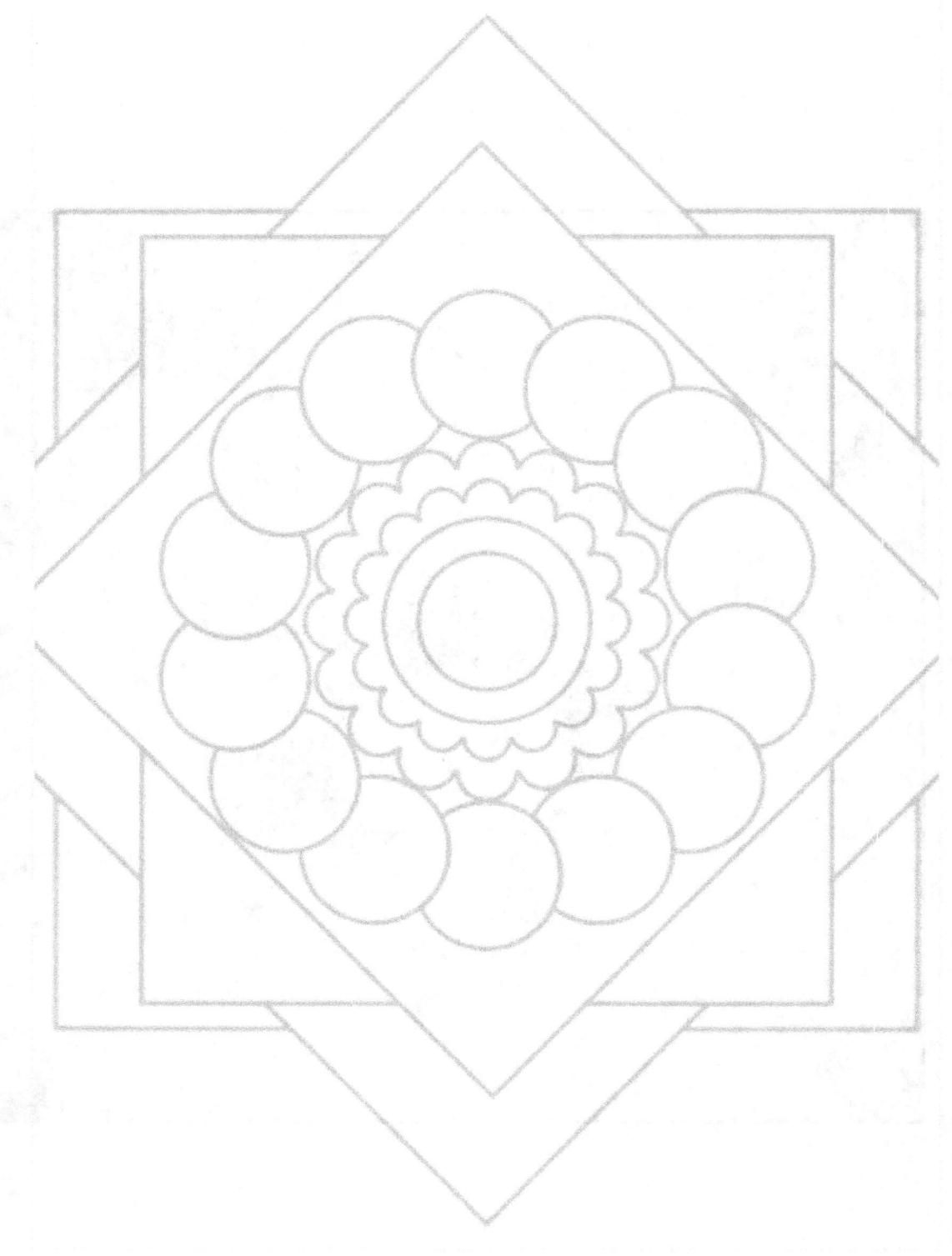

Copyrighted Material

Carnation

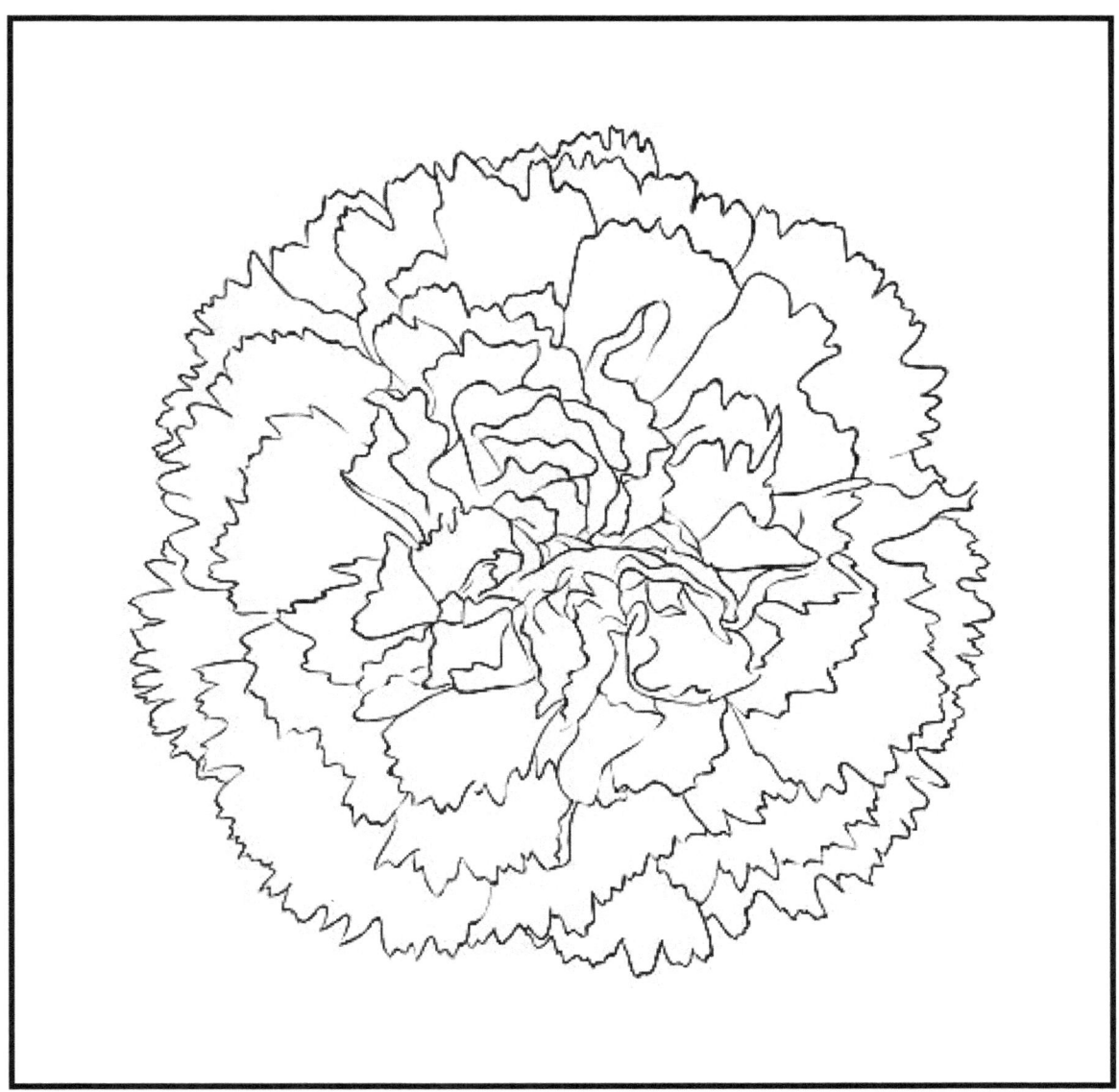

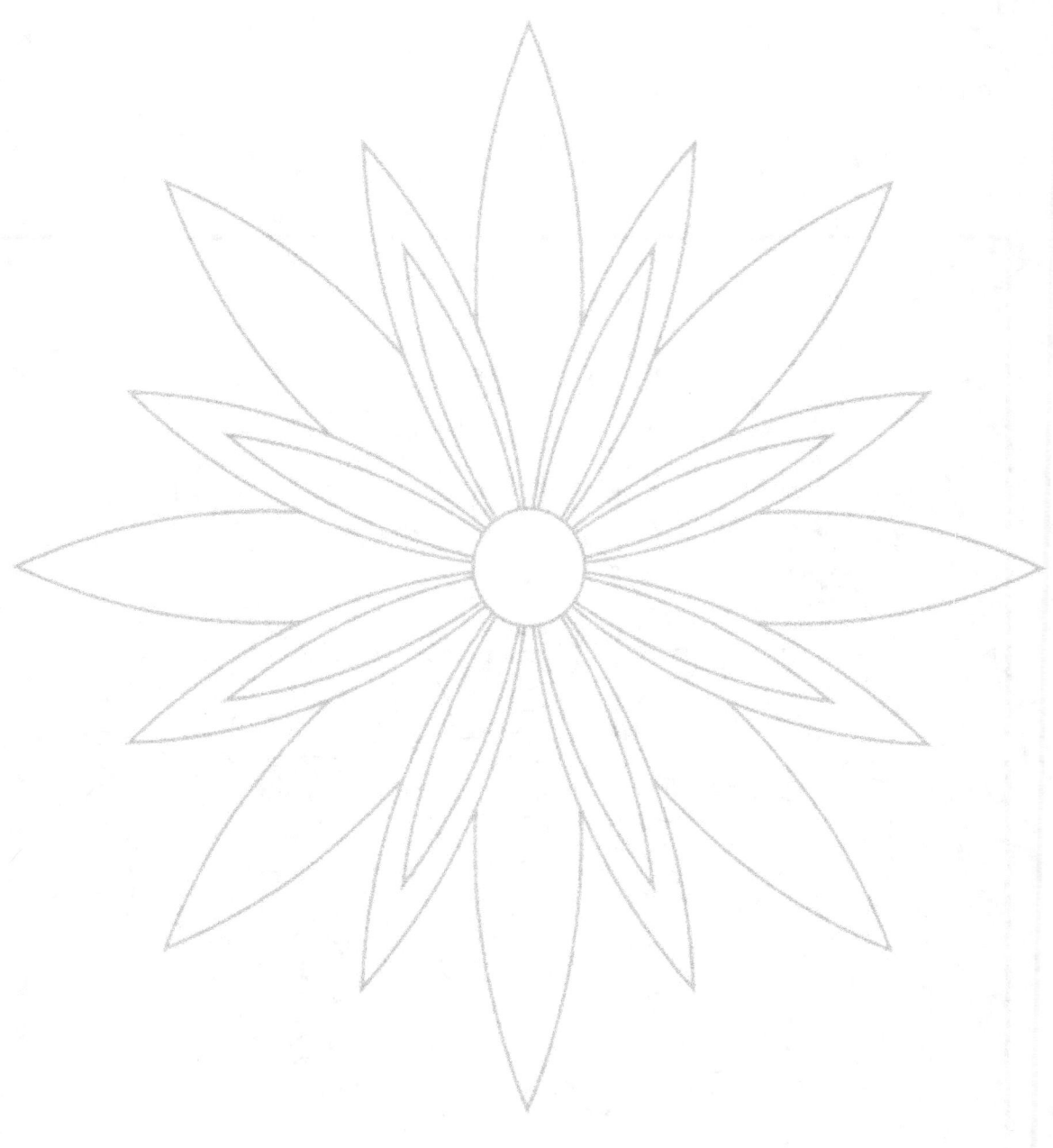

Copyrighted Material

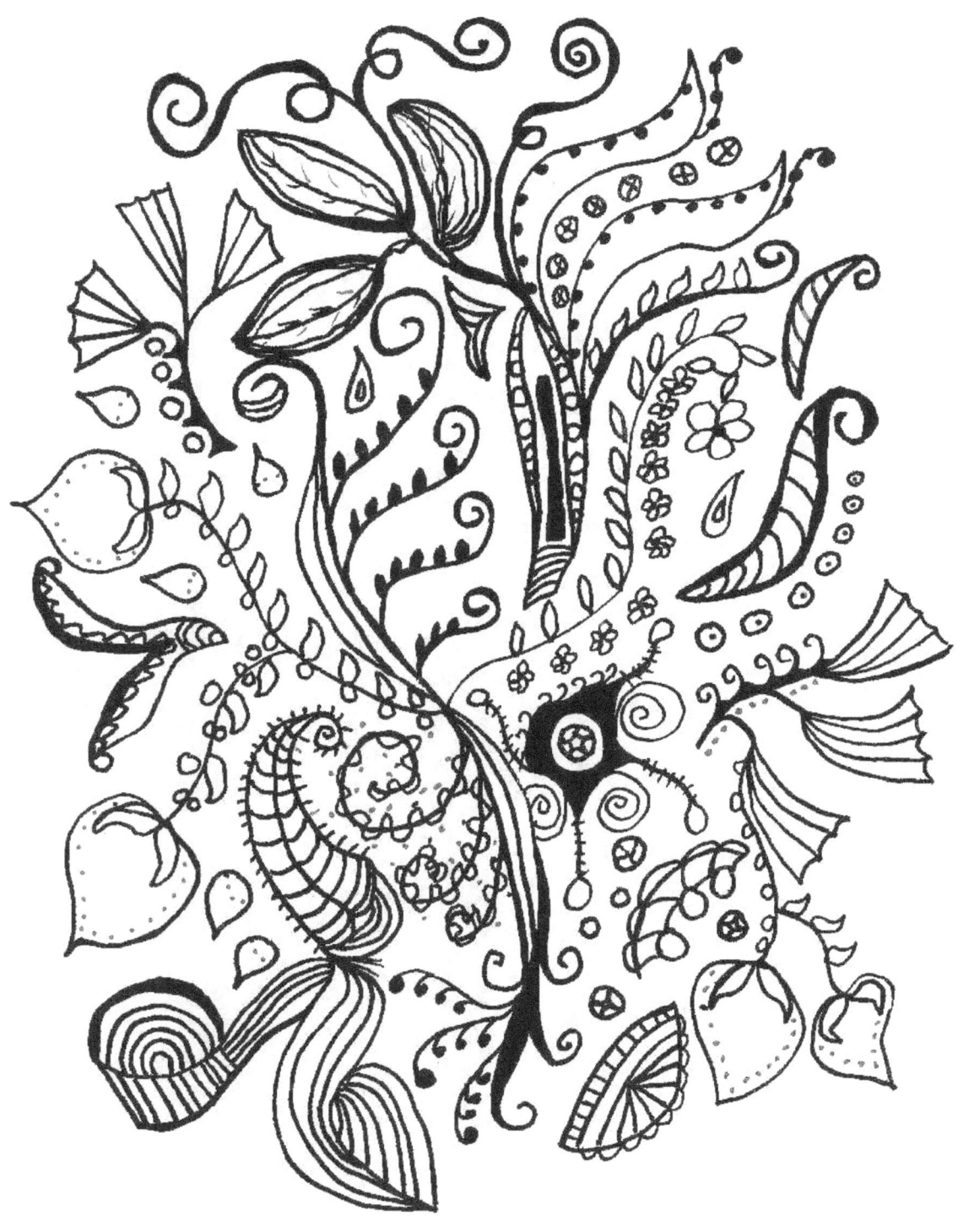

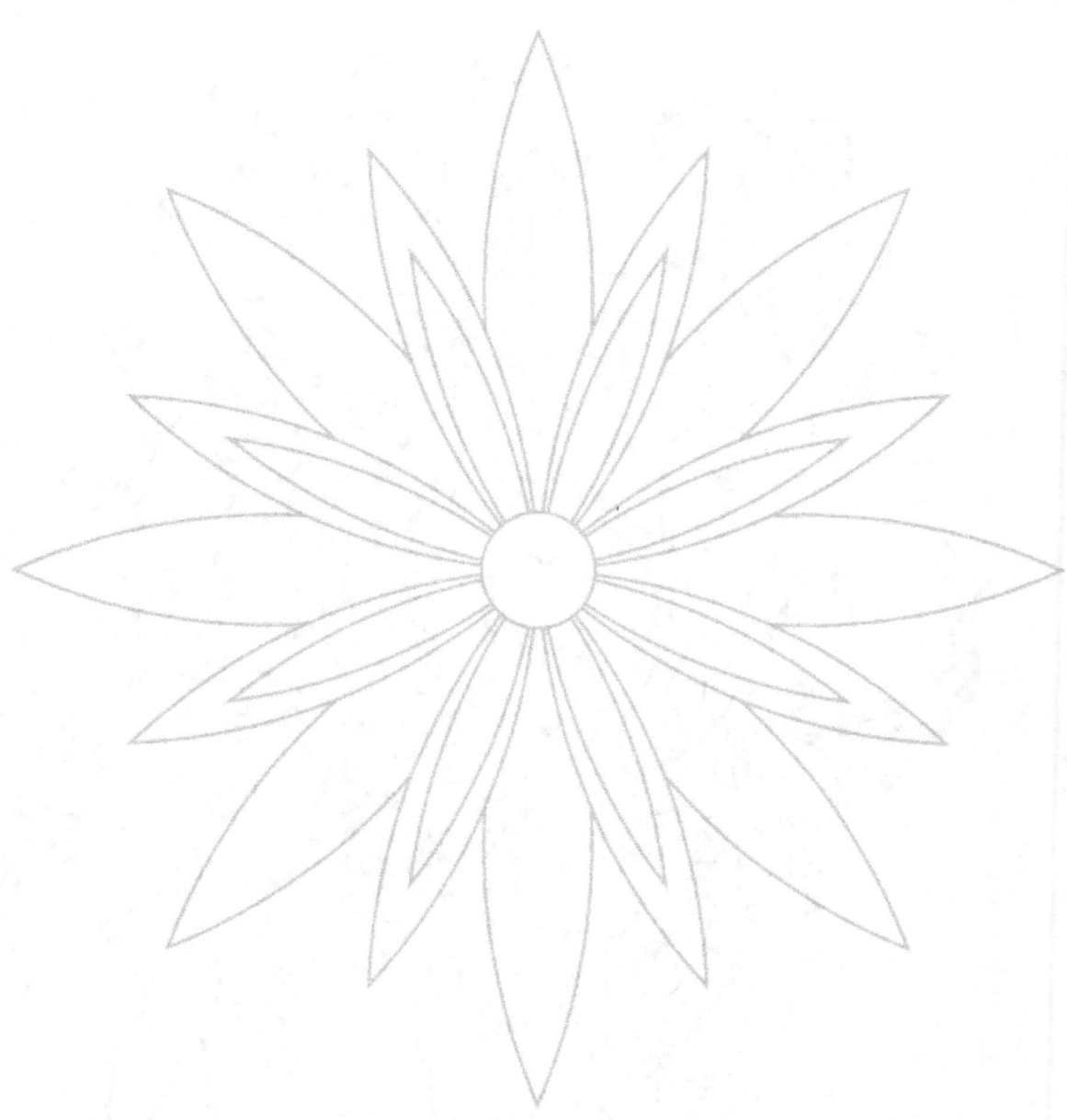

Rose

Copyrighted Material

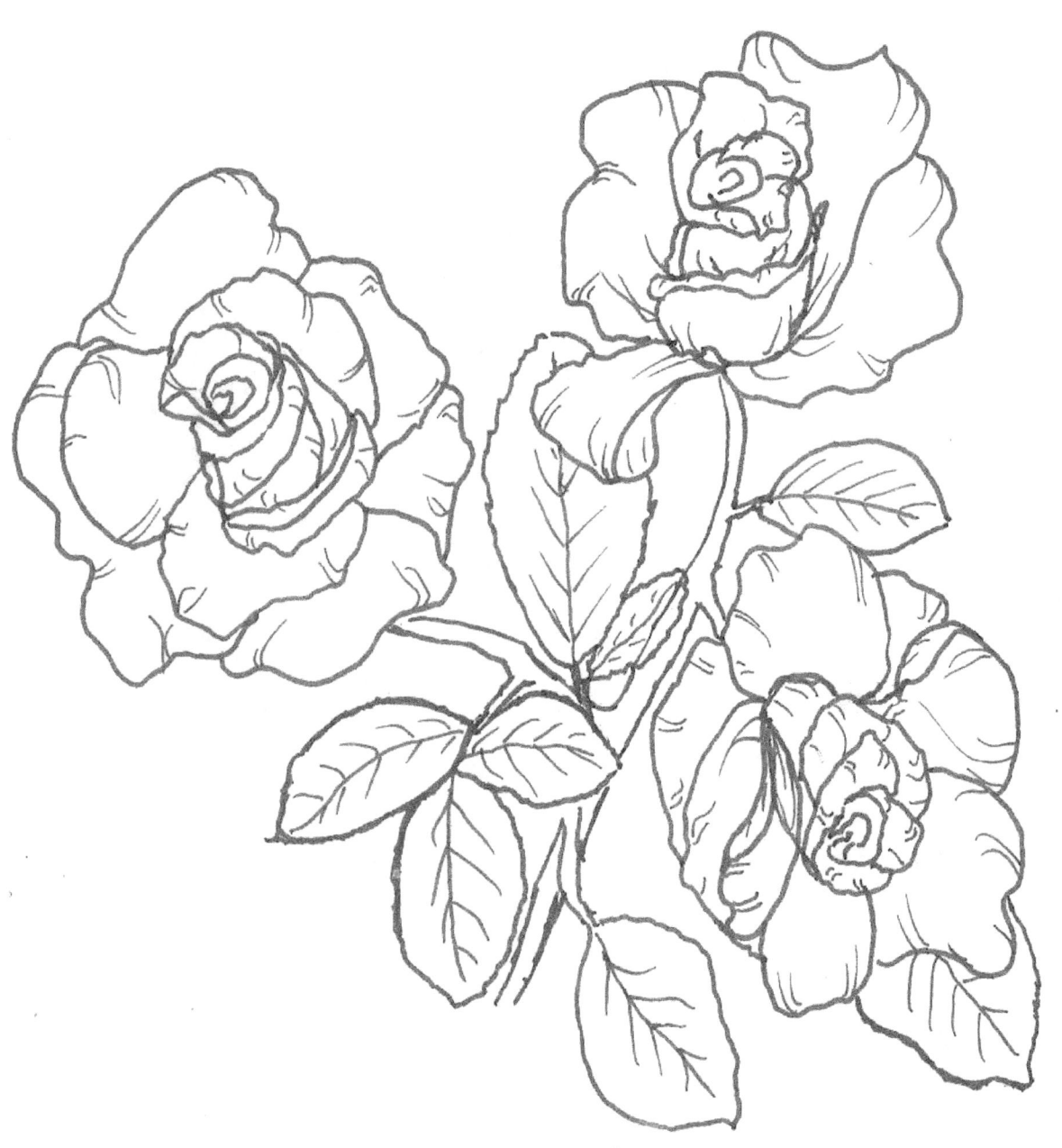

KD Coloring Studio

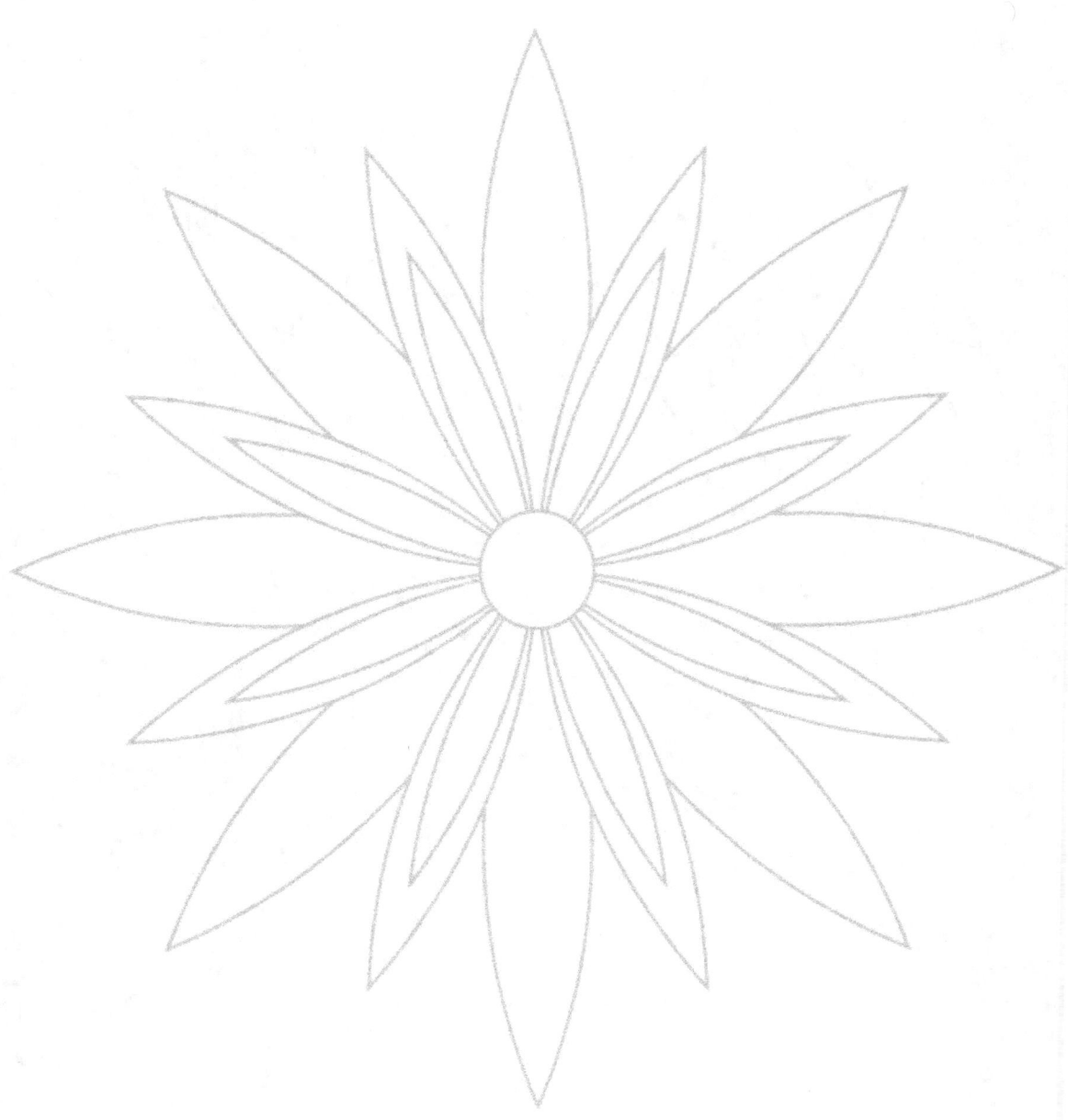

Poppy

Copyrighted Material

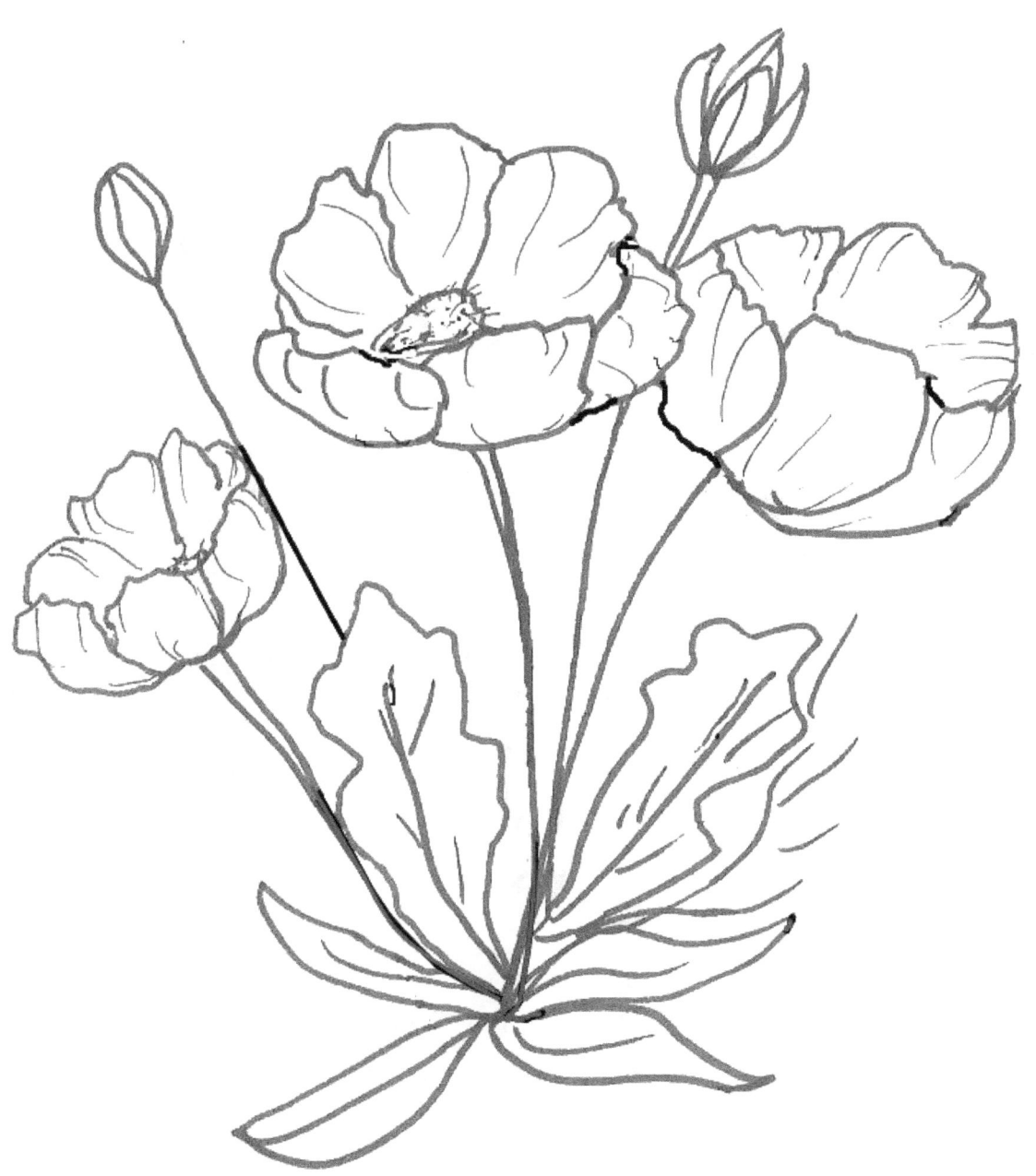

KD Coloring Studio

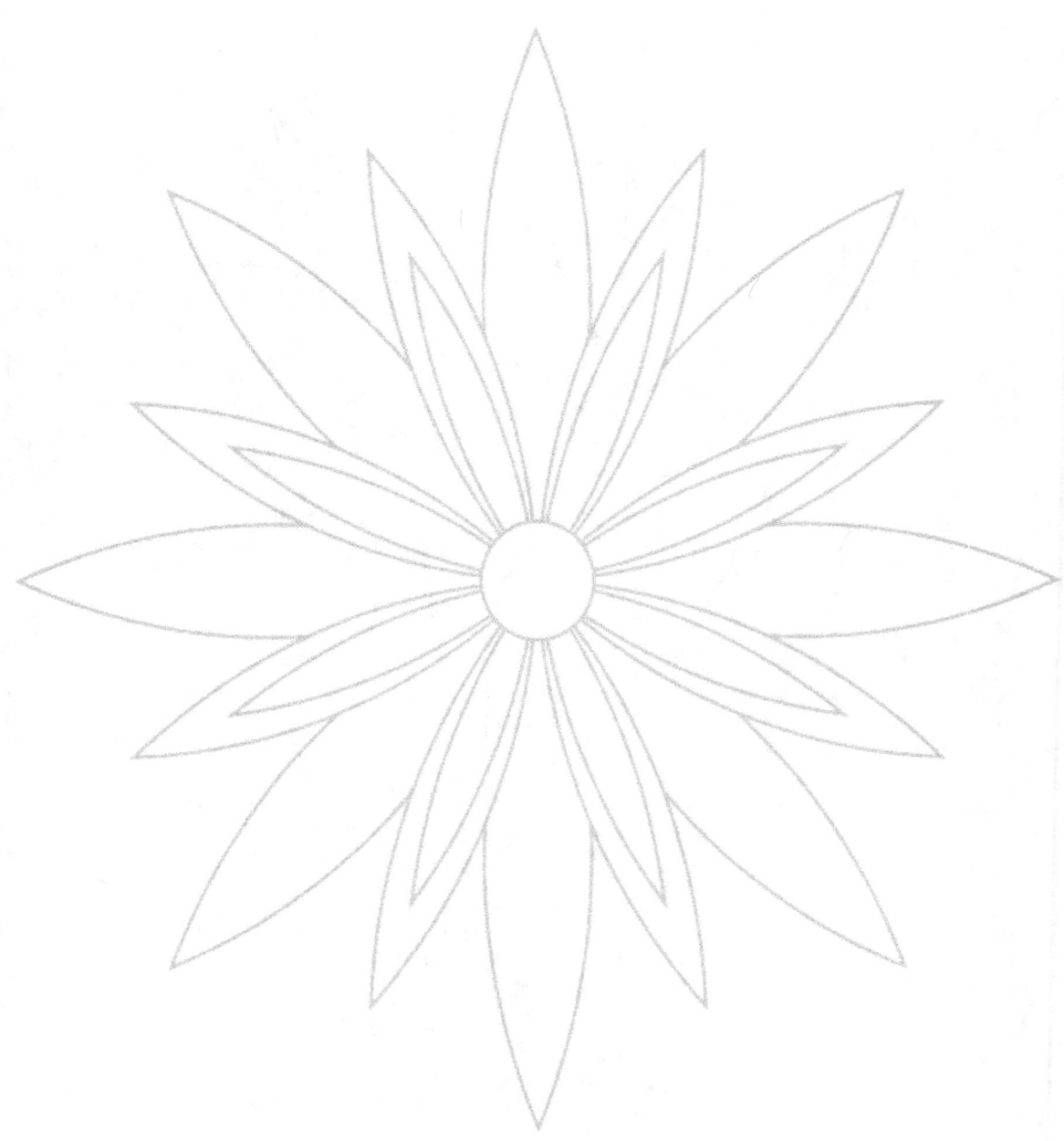

Copyrighted Material

Peony

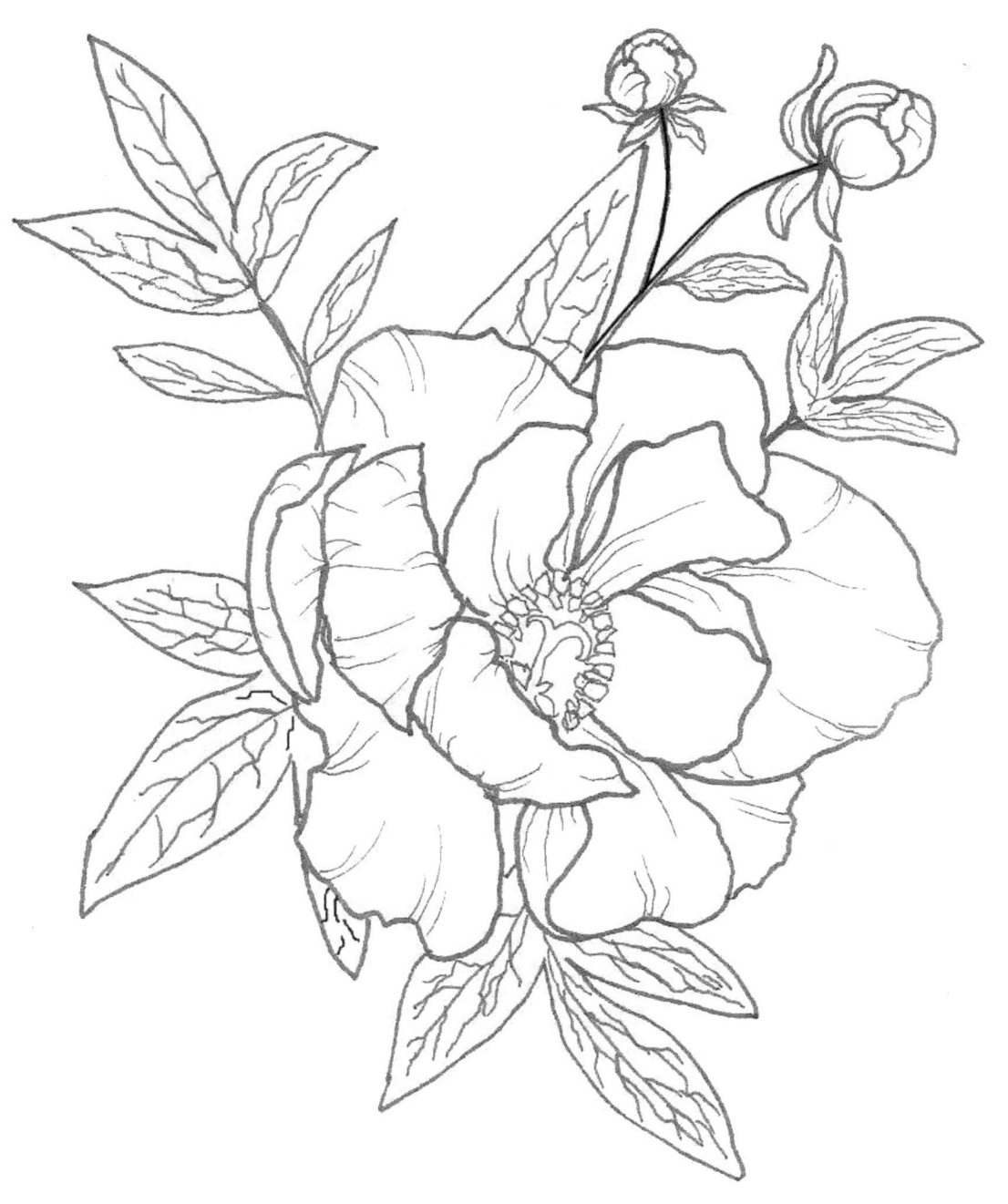

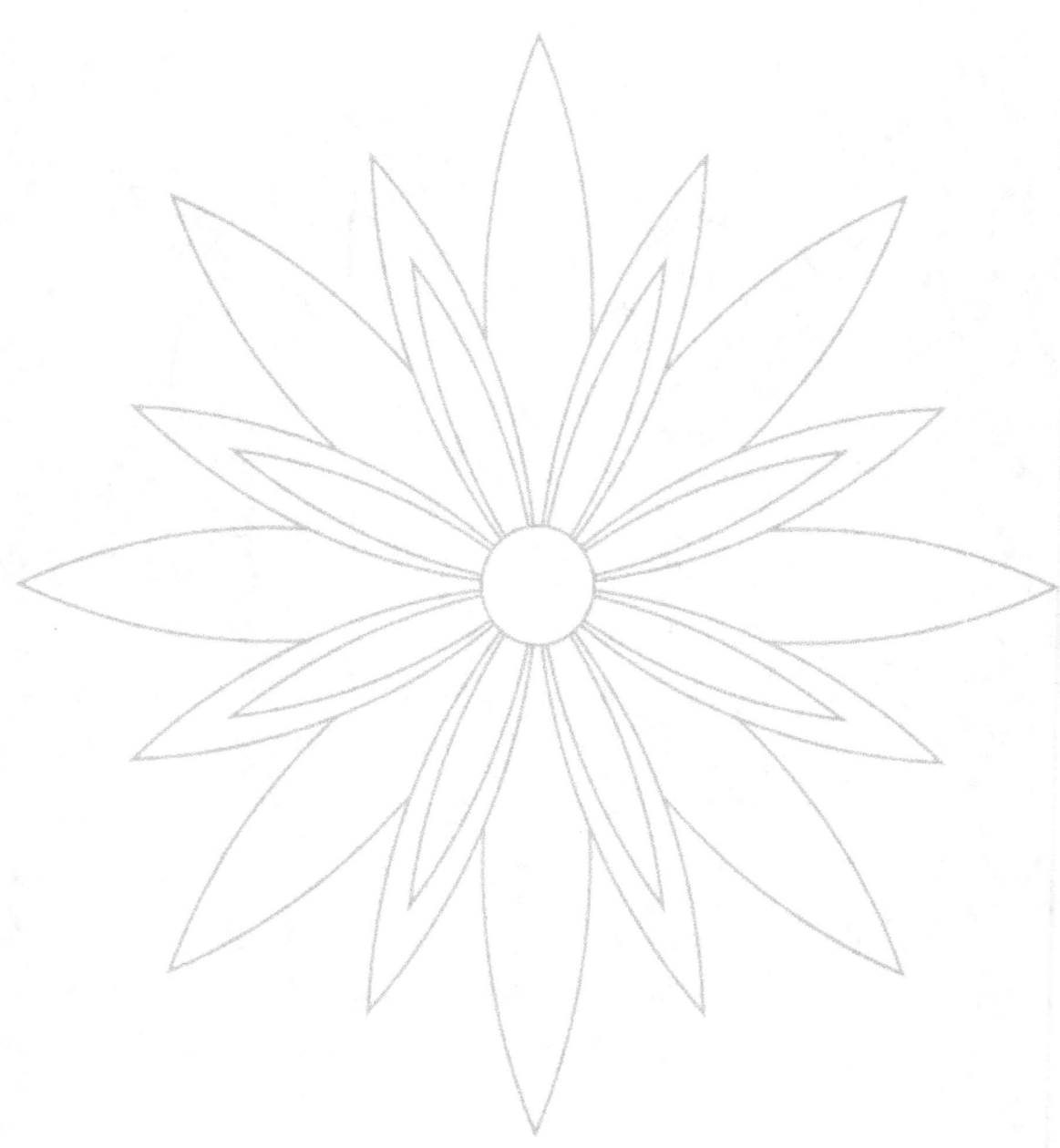

Copyrighted Material

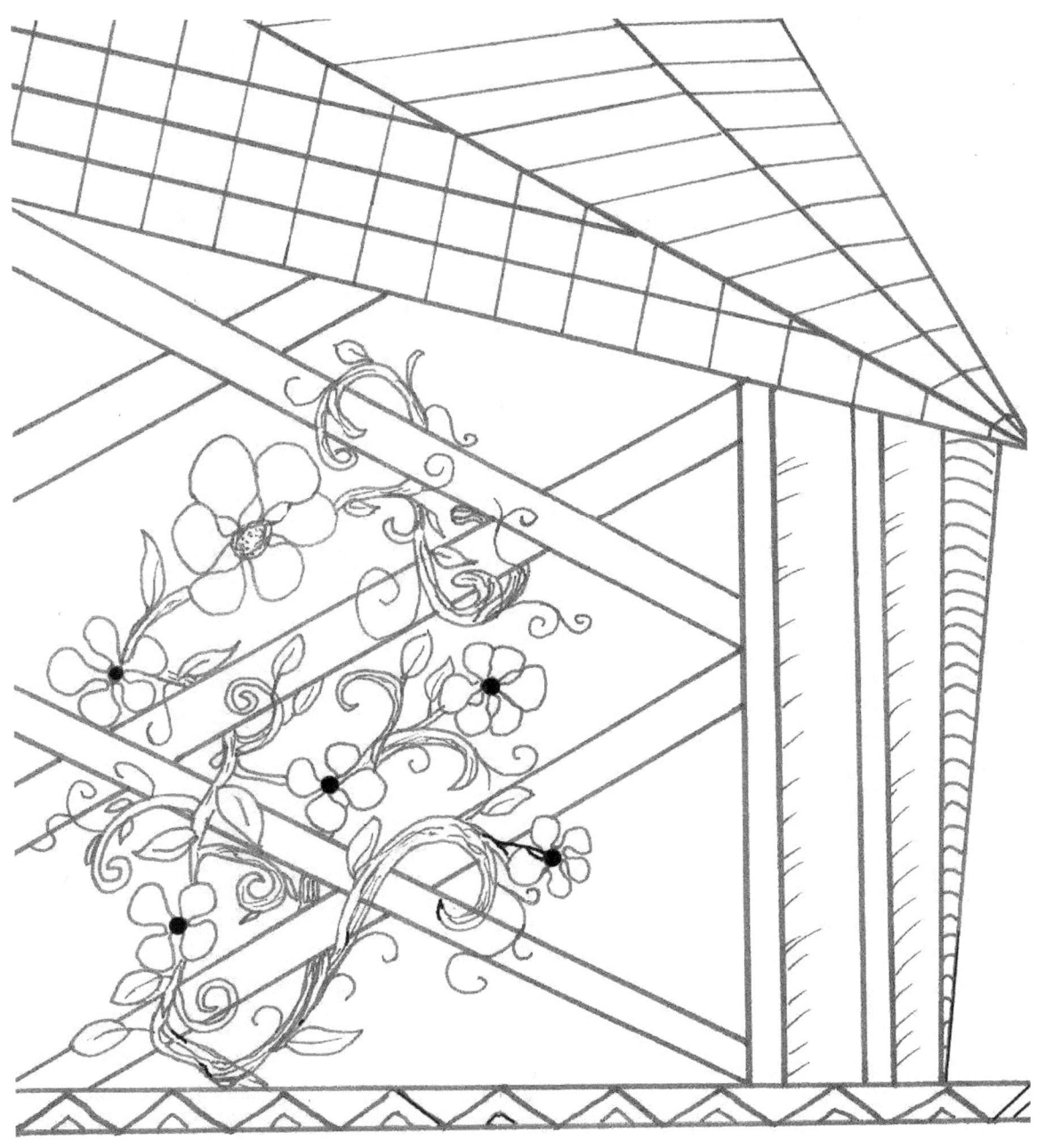

KD Coloring Studio

Copyrighted Material

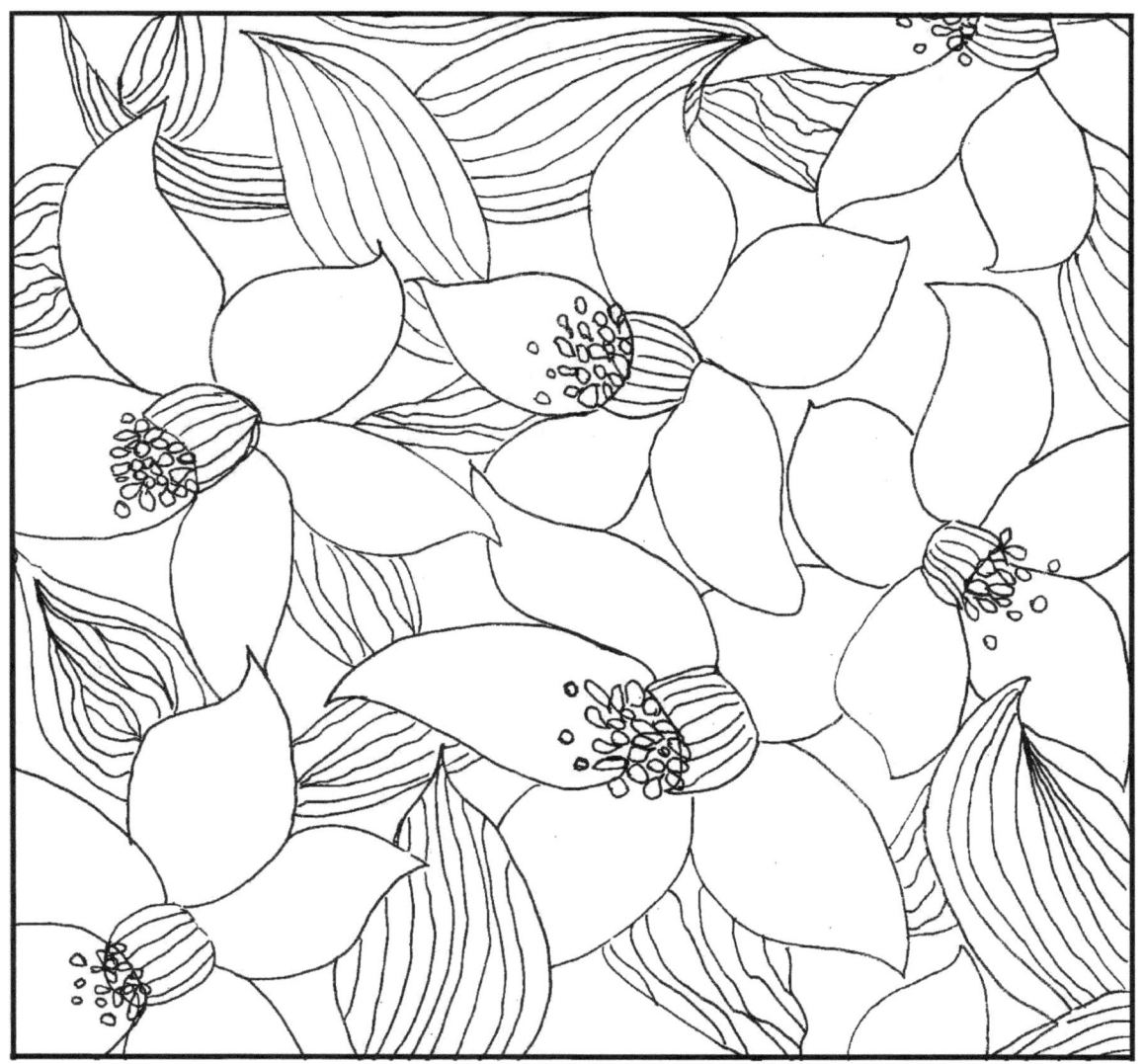

KD Coloring Studio

Copyrighted Material

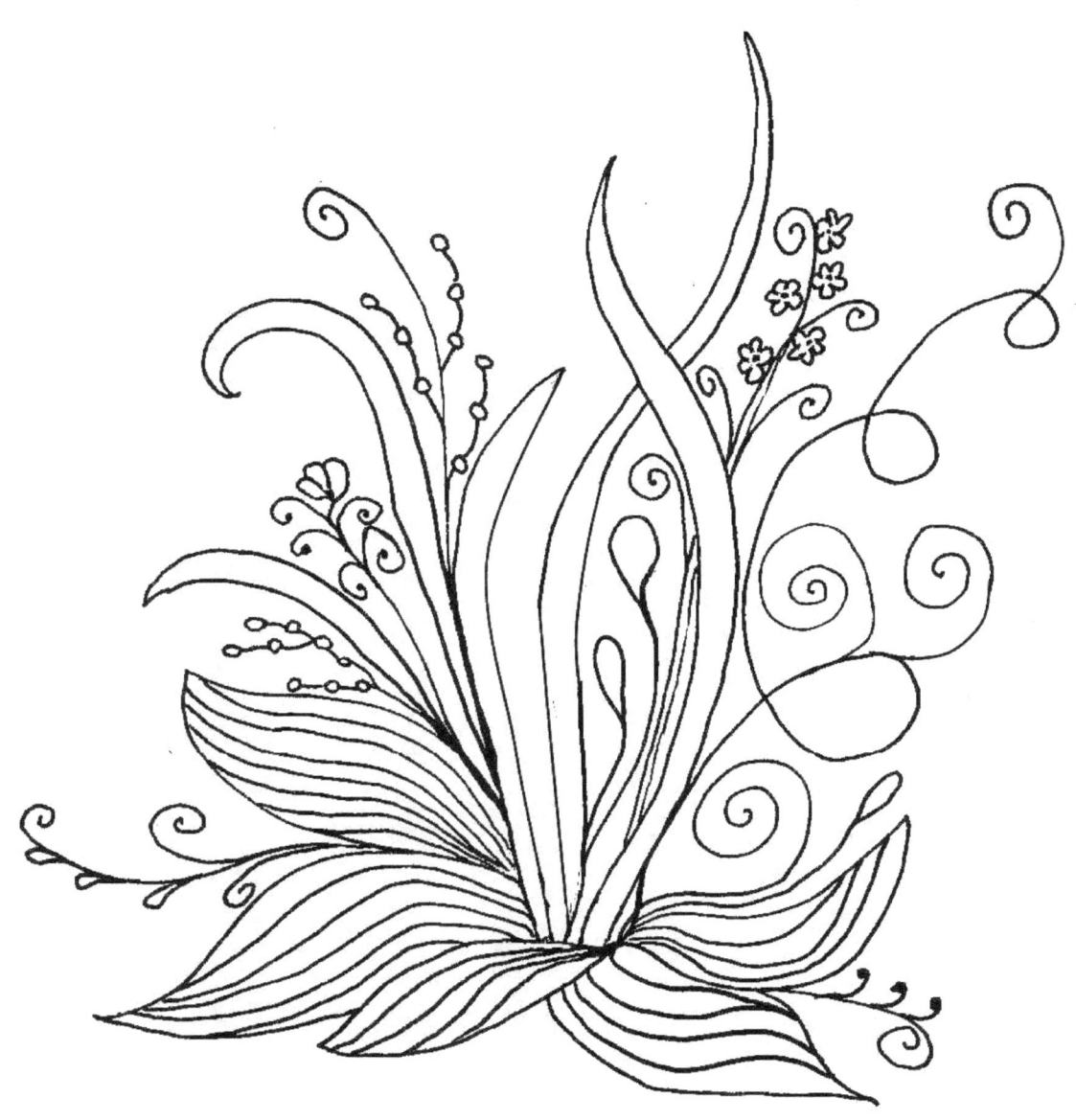

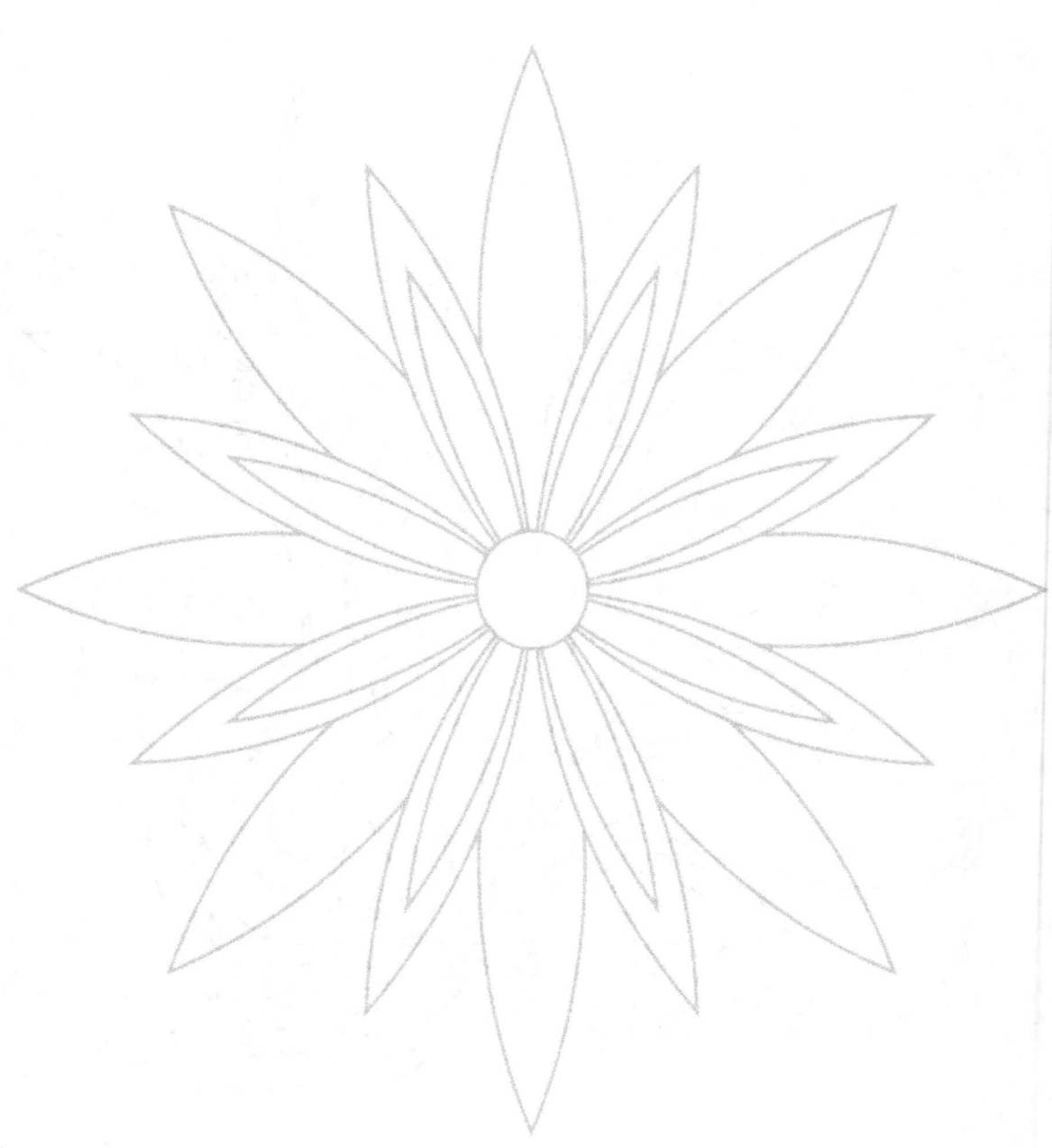

Copyrighted Material

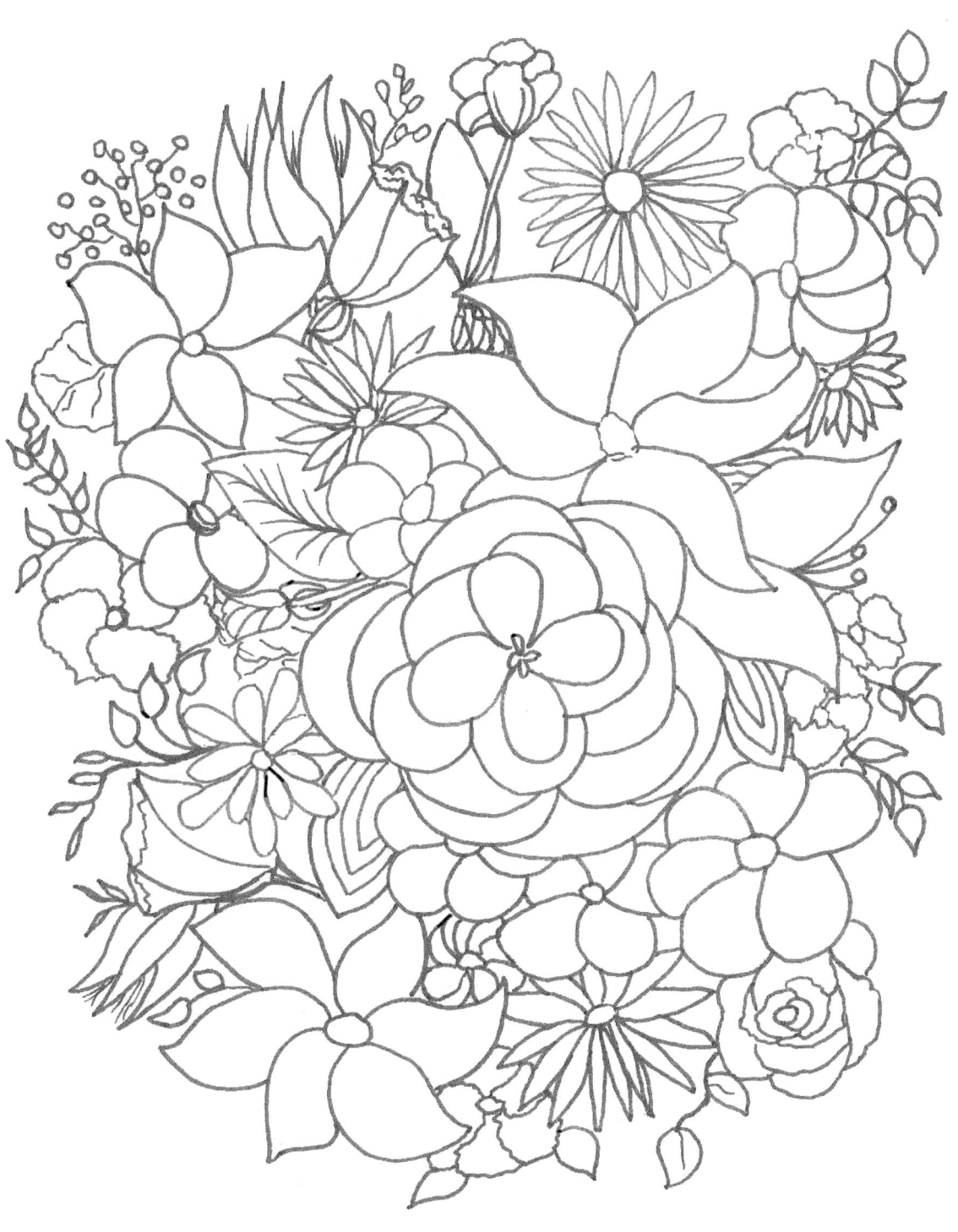

KD Coloring Studio

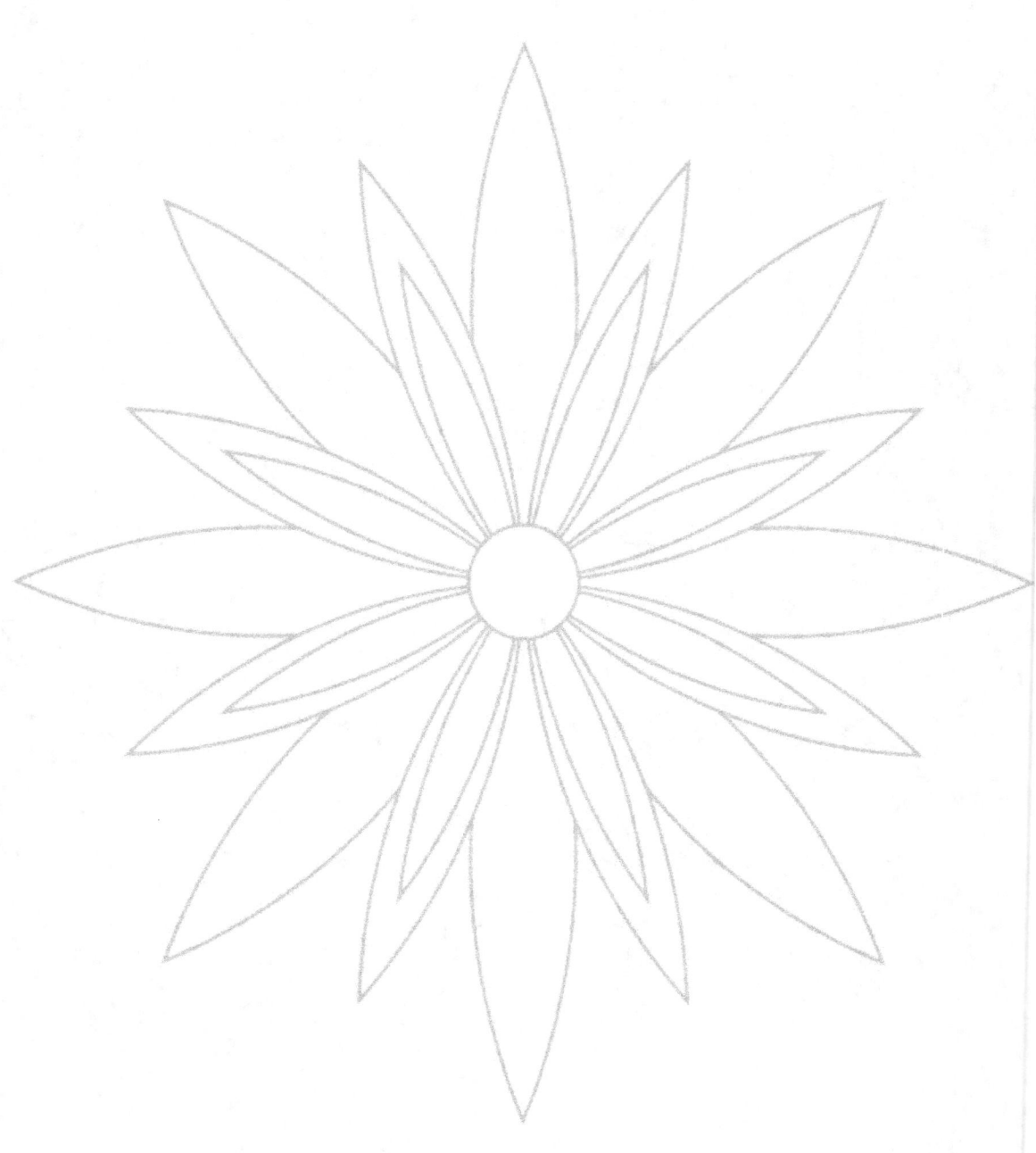

Copyrighted Material

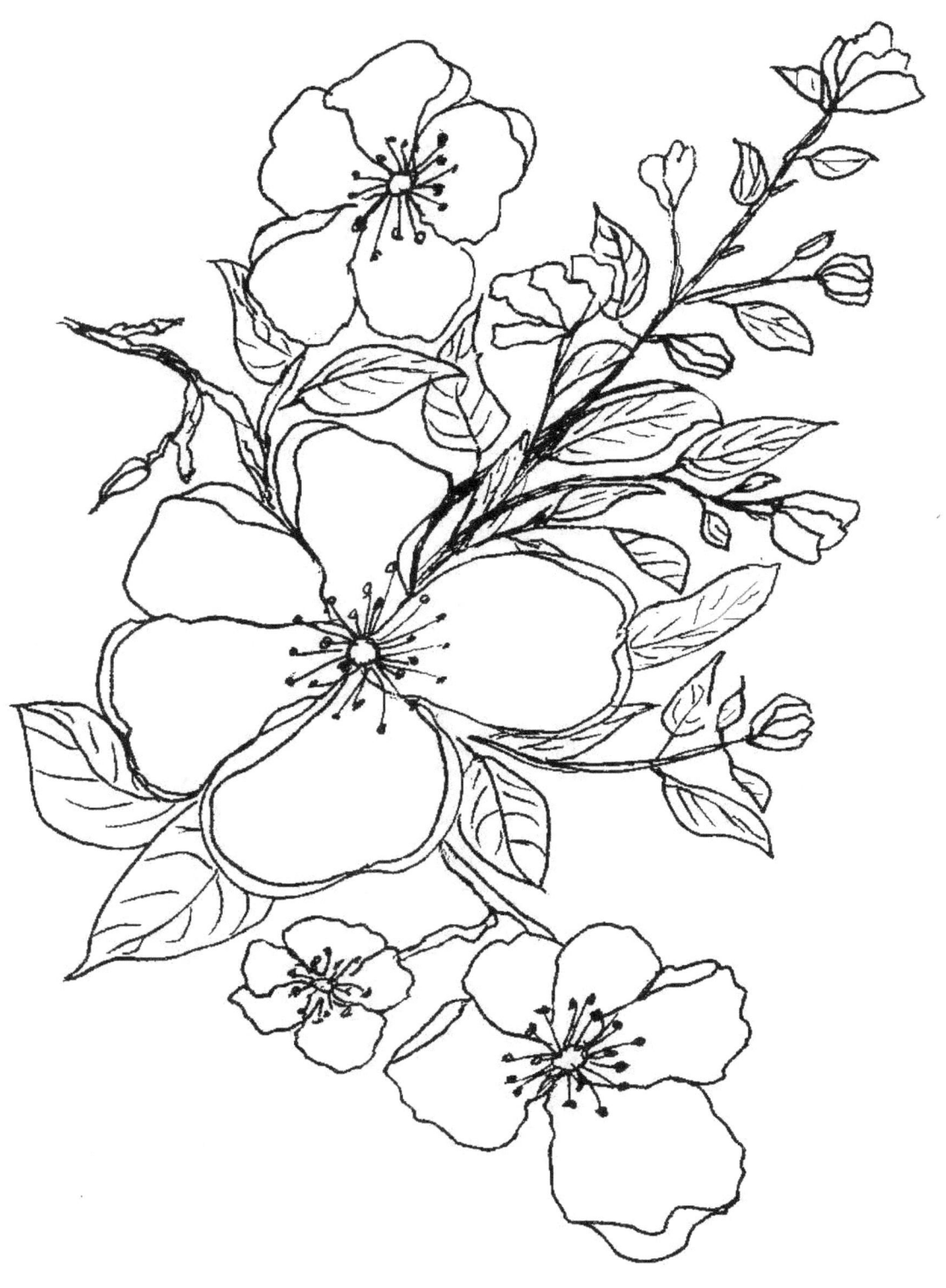

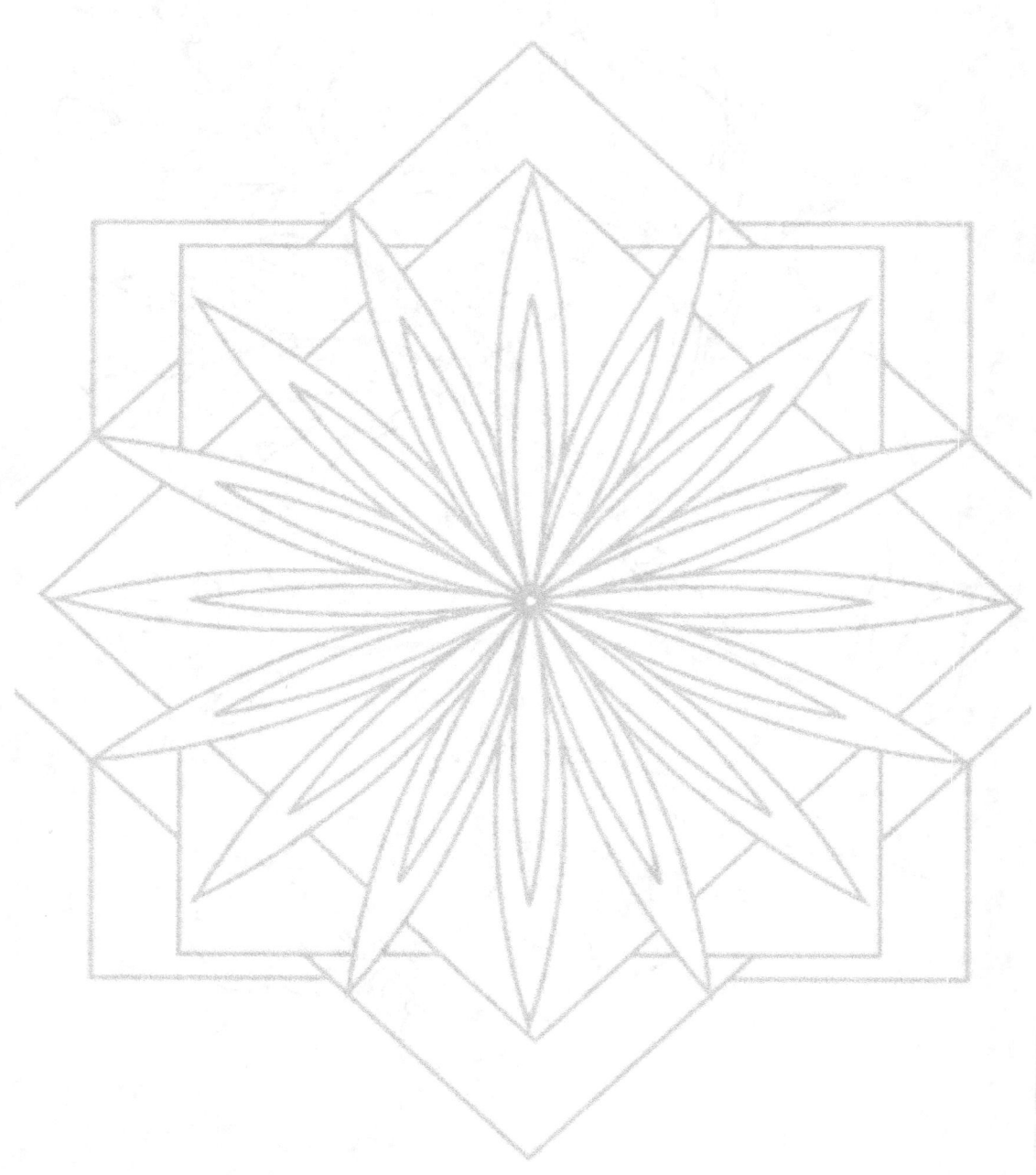

Copyrighted Material

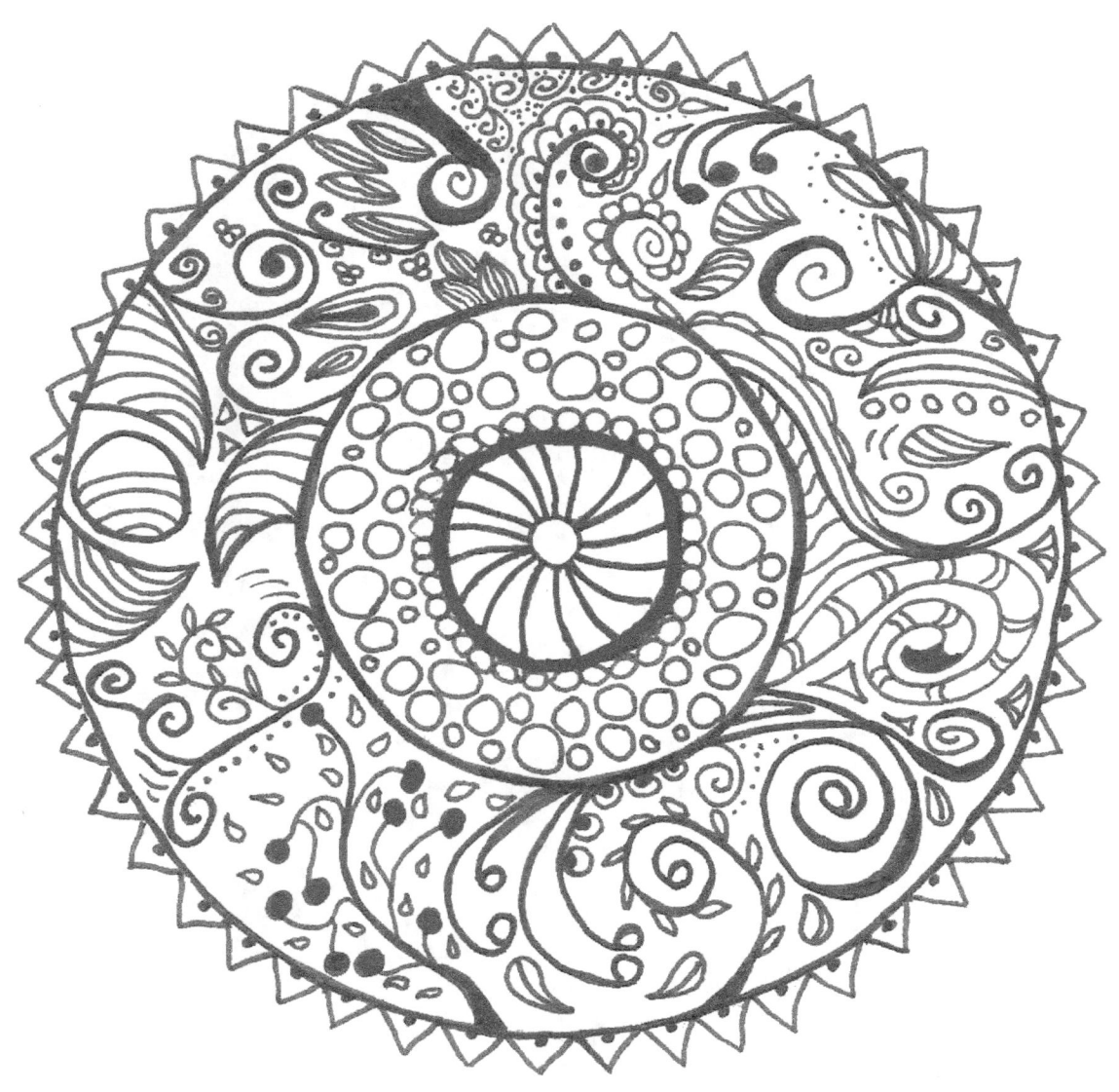

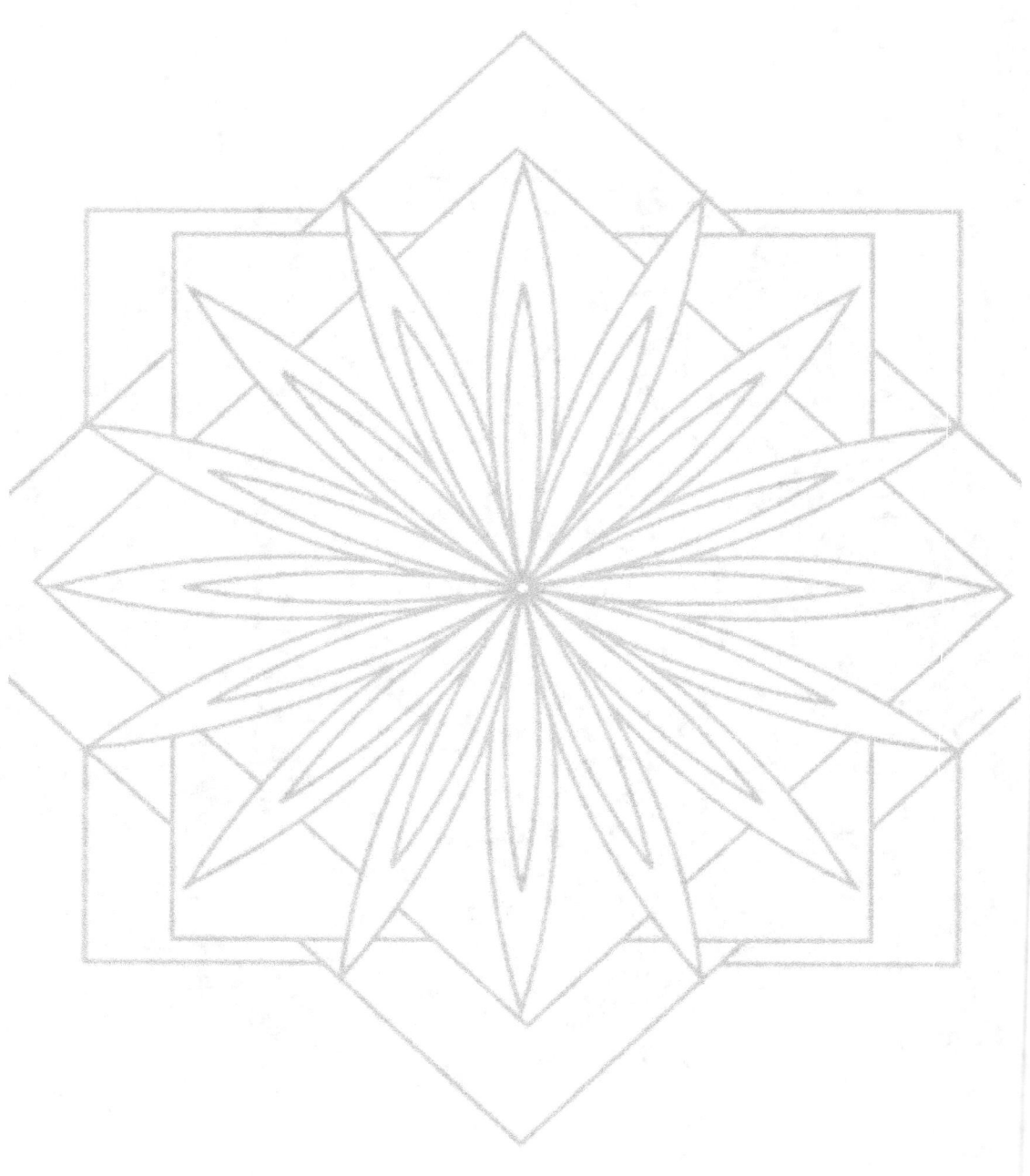

Copyrighted Material

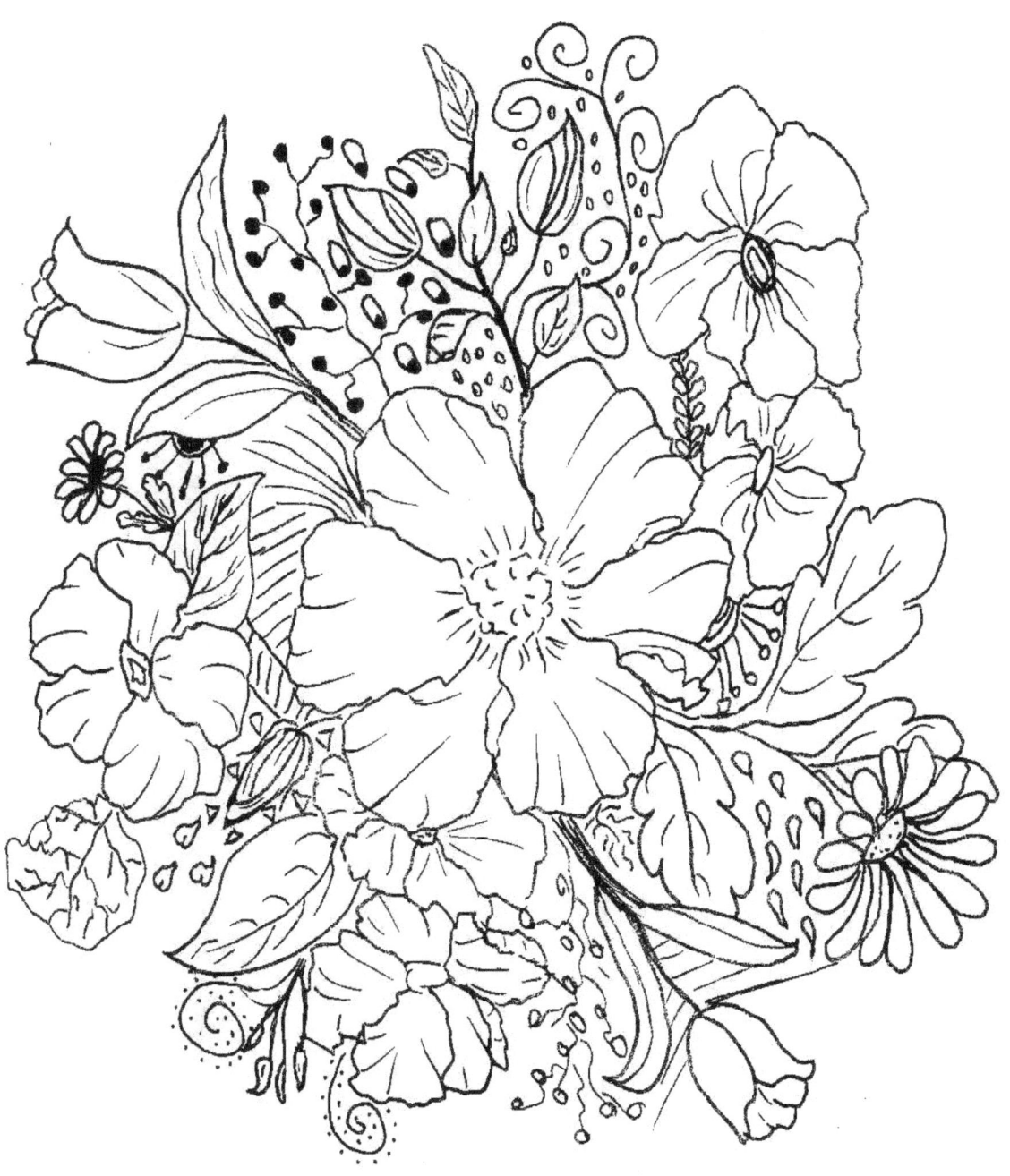

KD Coloring Studio

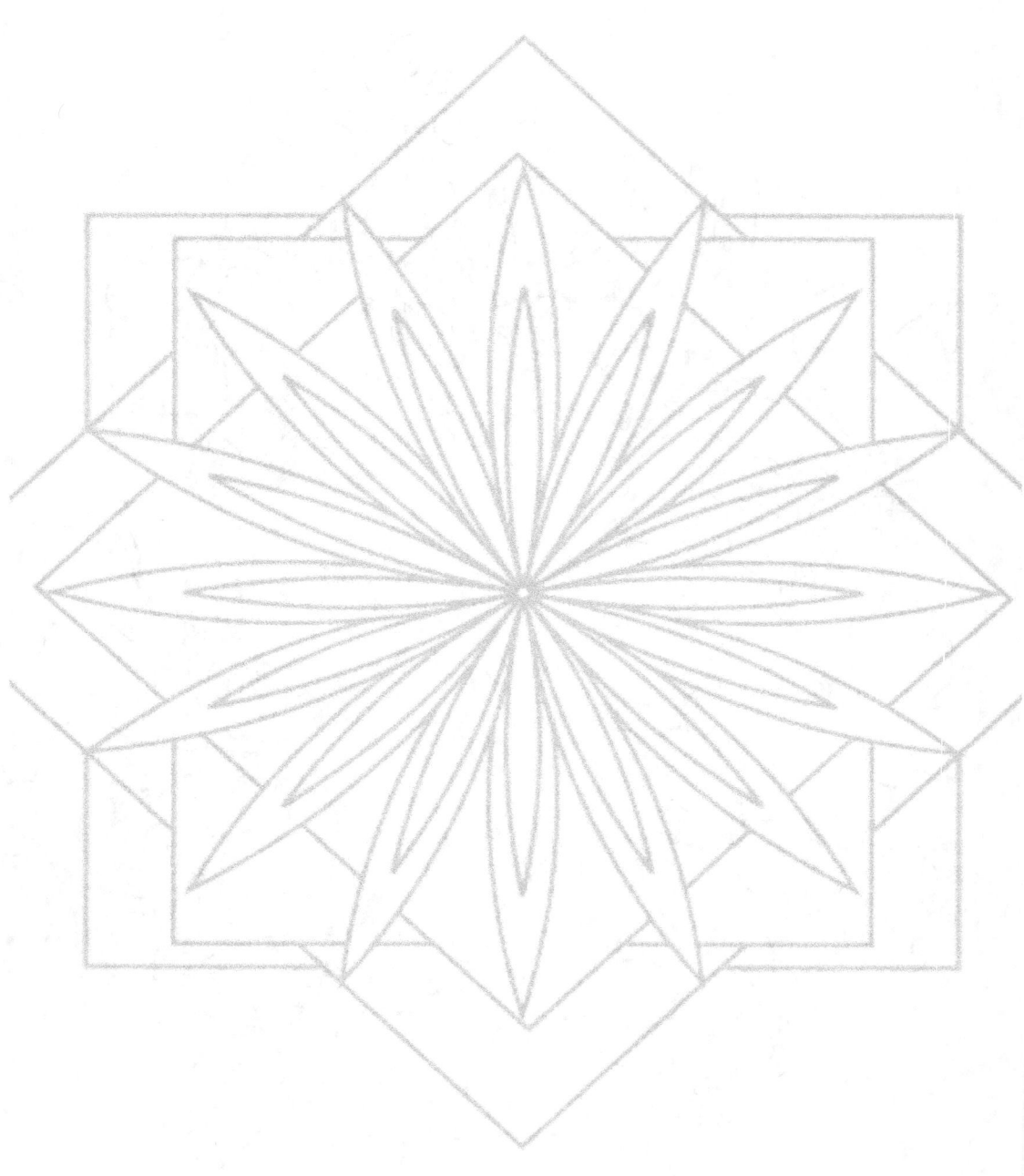

Copyrighted Material

Hibiscus

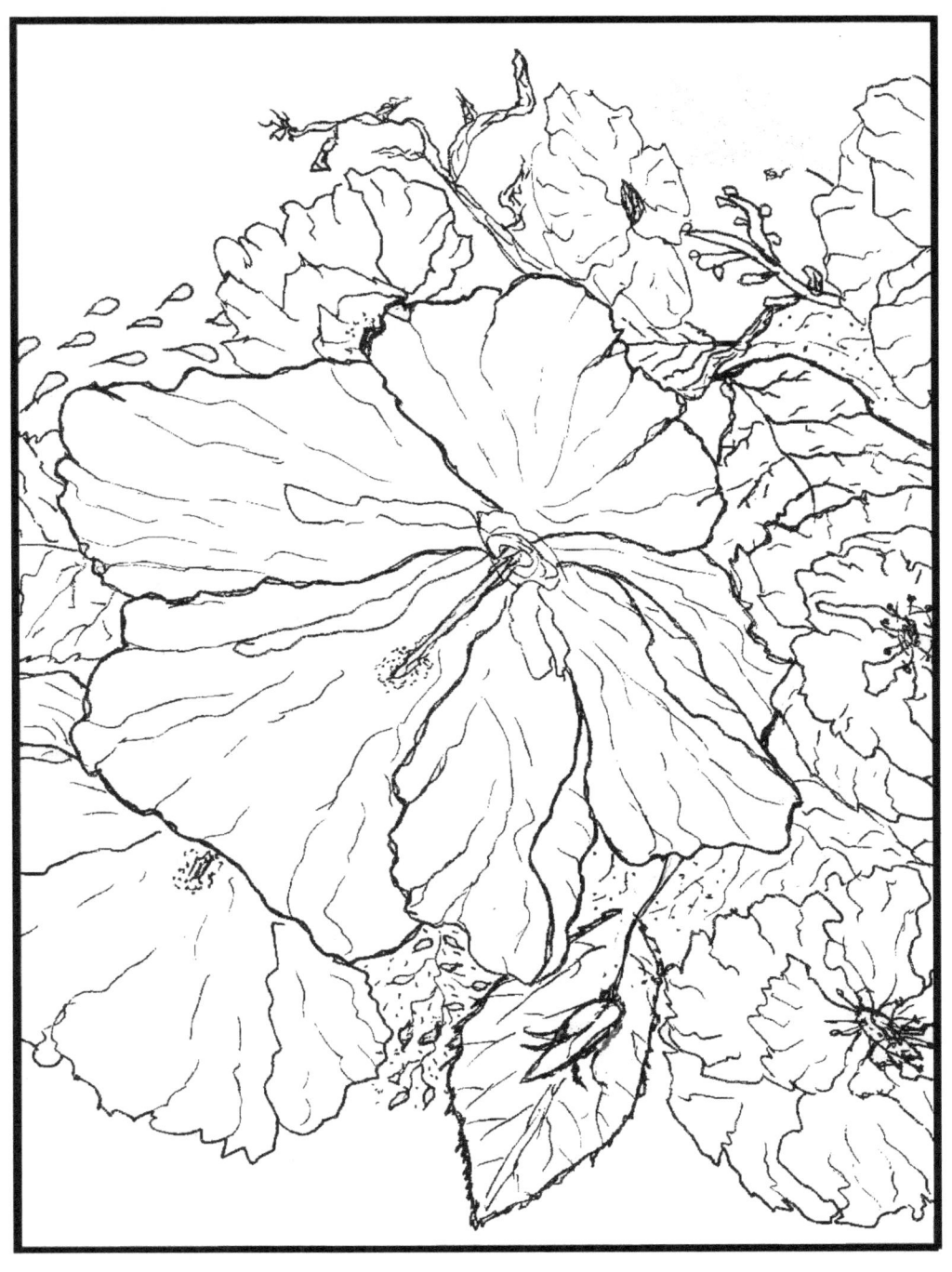

KD Coloring Studio

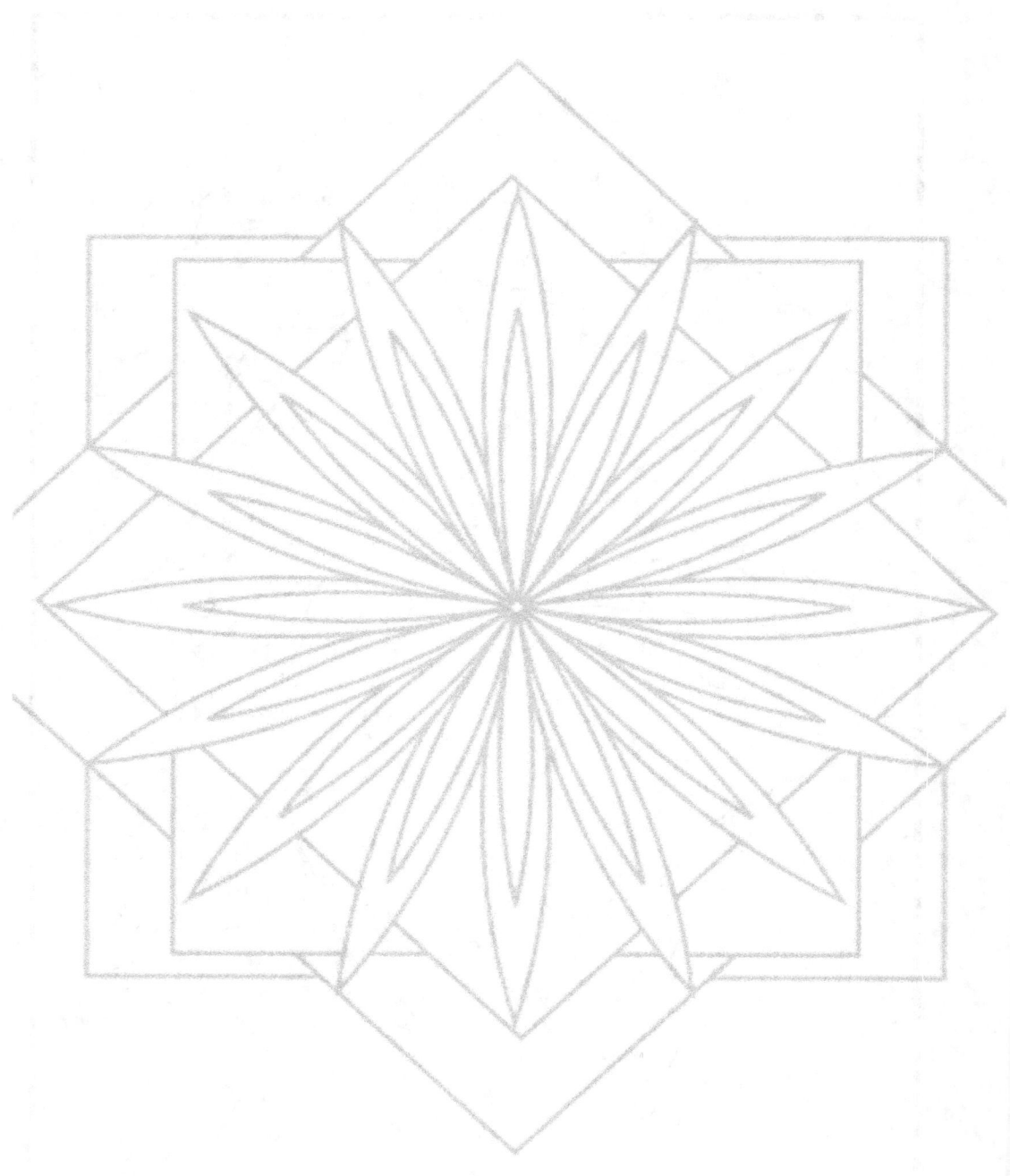

Copyrighted Material

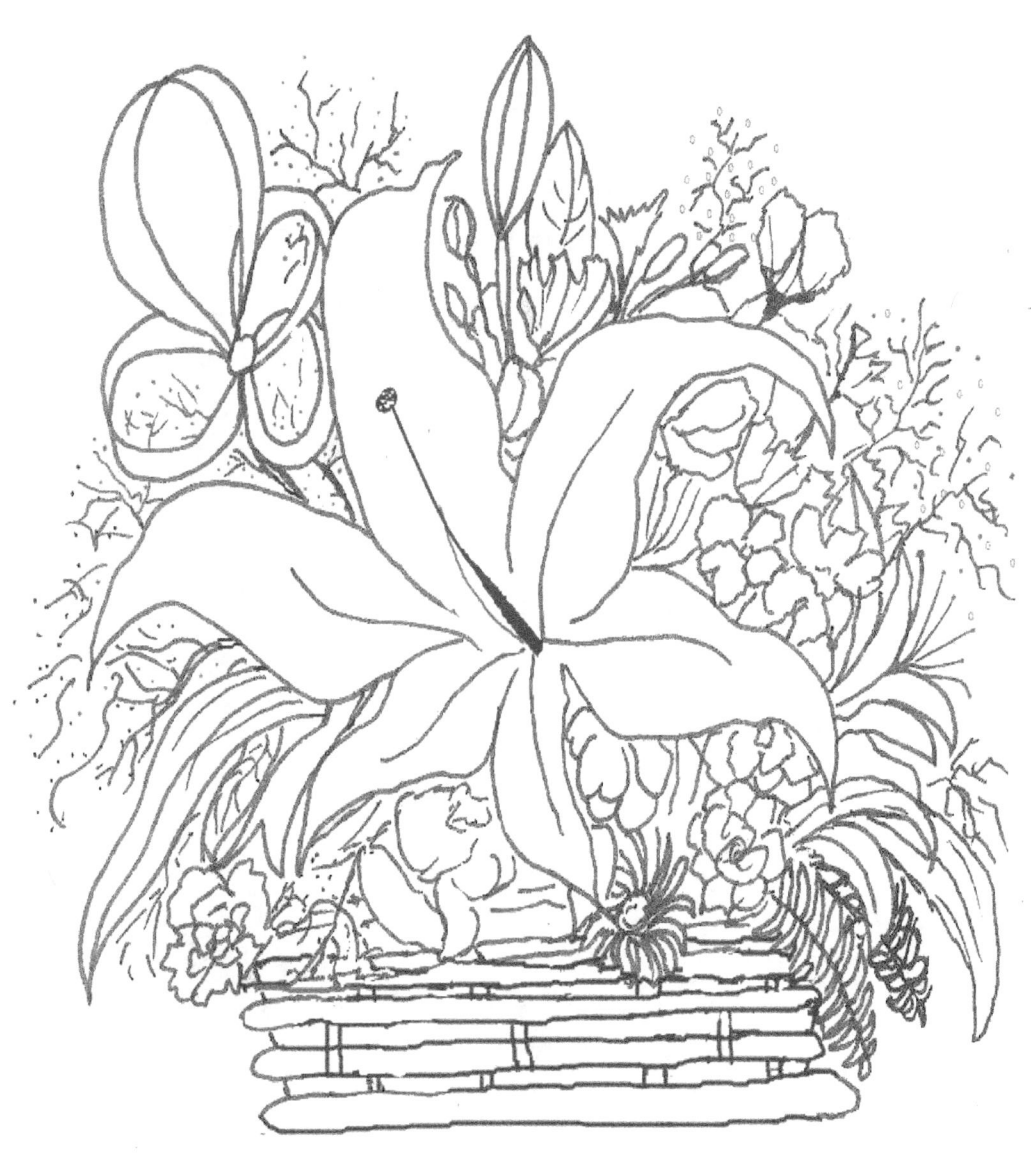

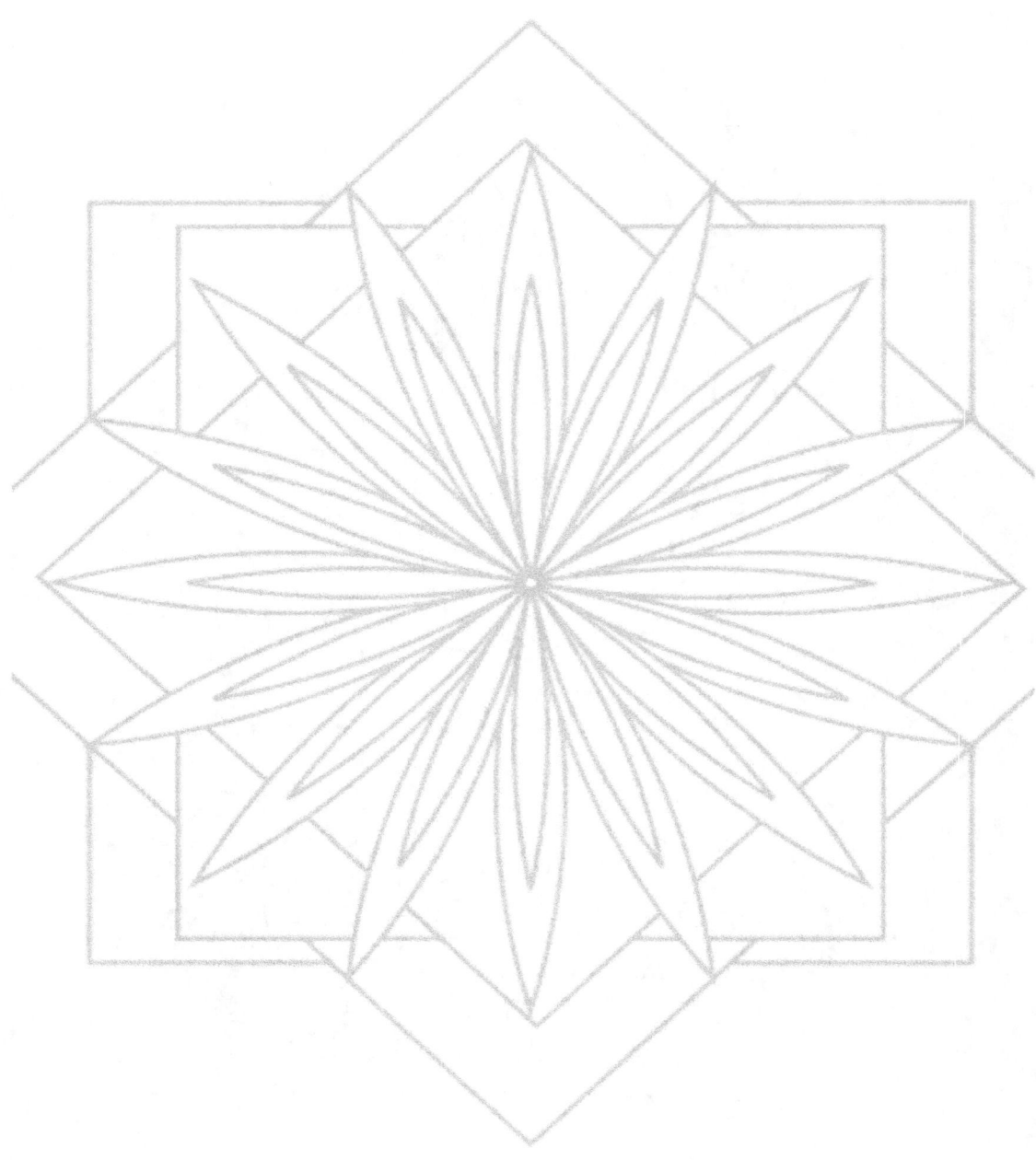

Copyrighted Material

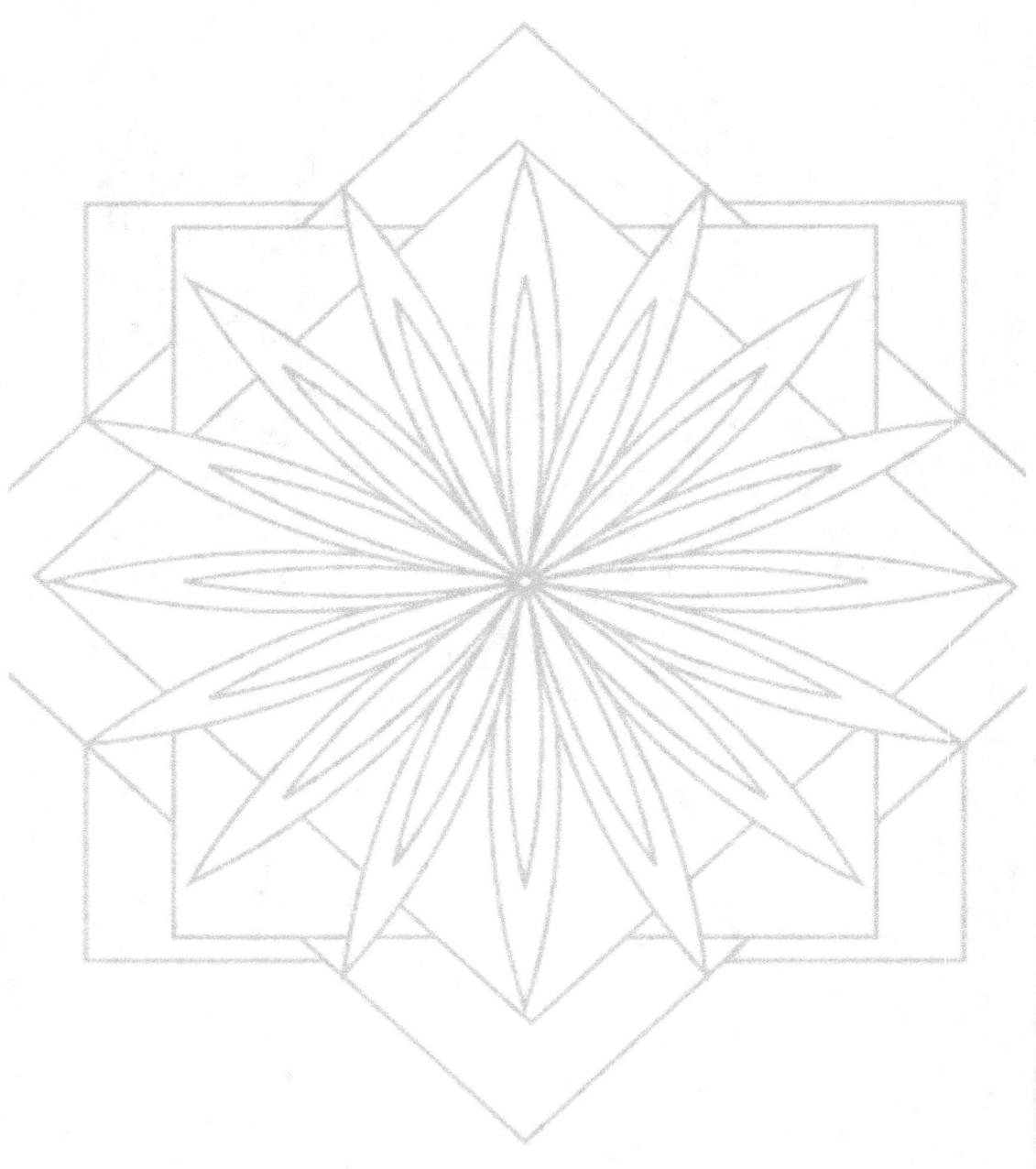

Copyrighted Material

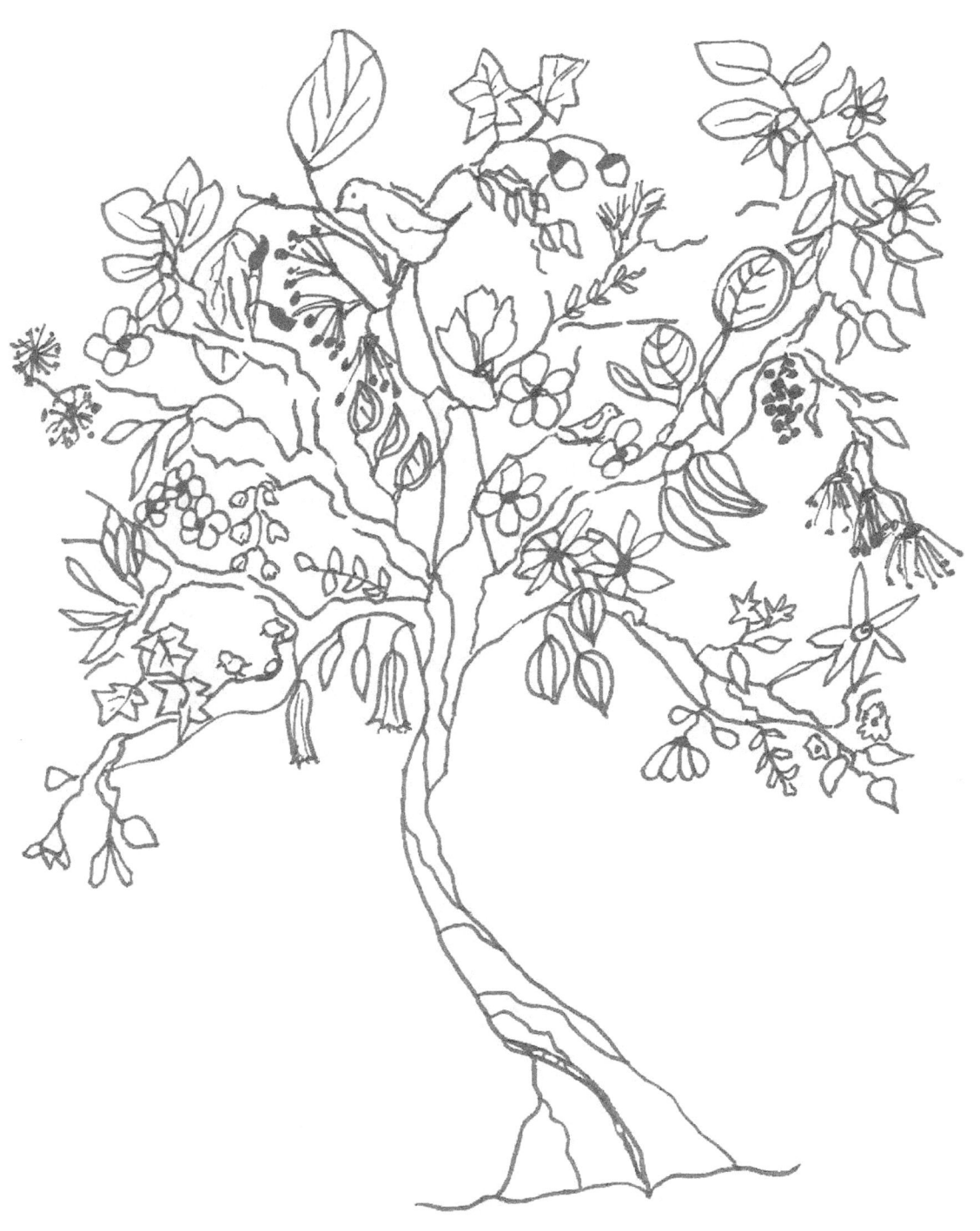

KD Coloring Studio

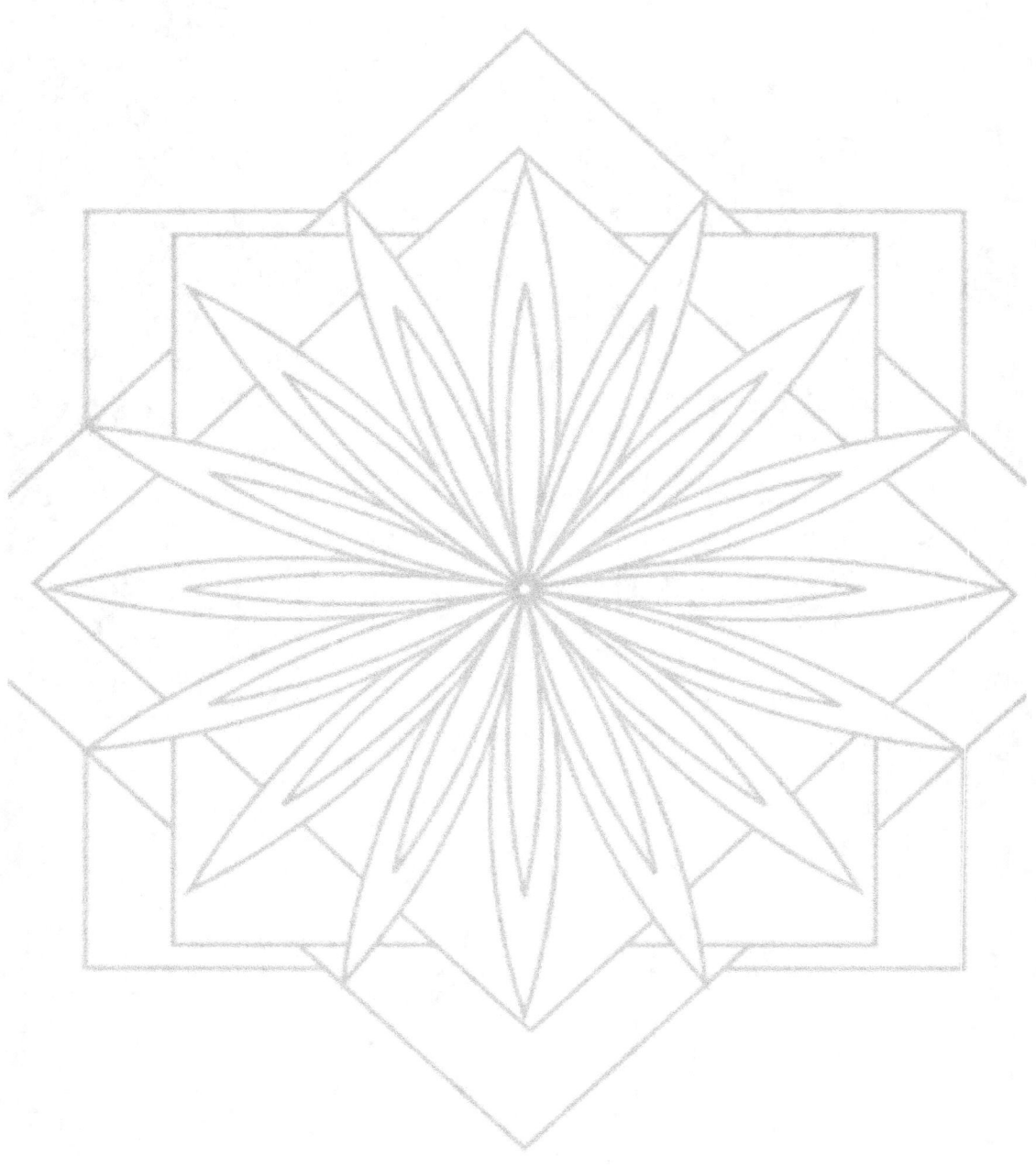

Copyrighted Material

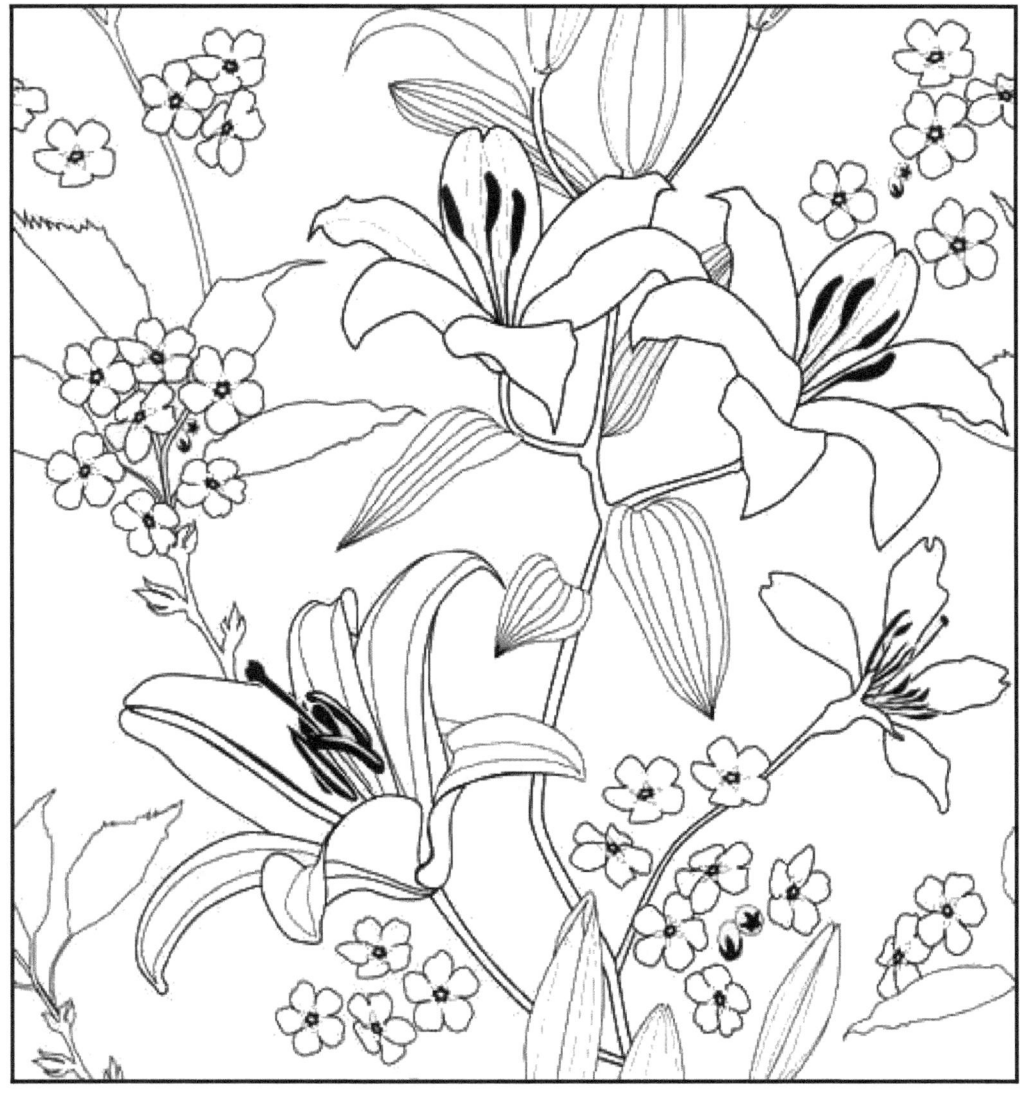

KD Coloring Studio

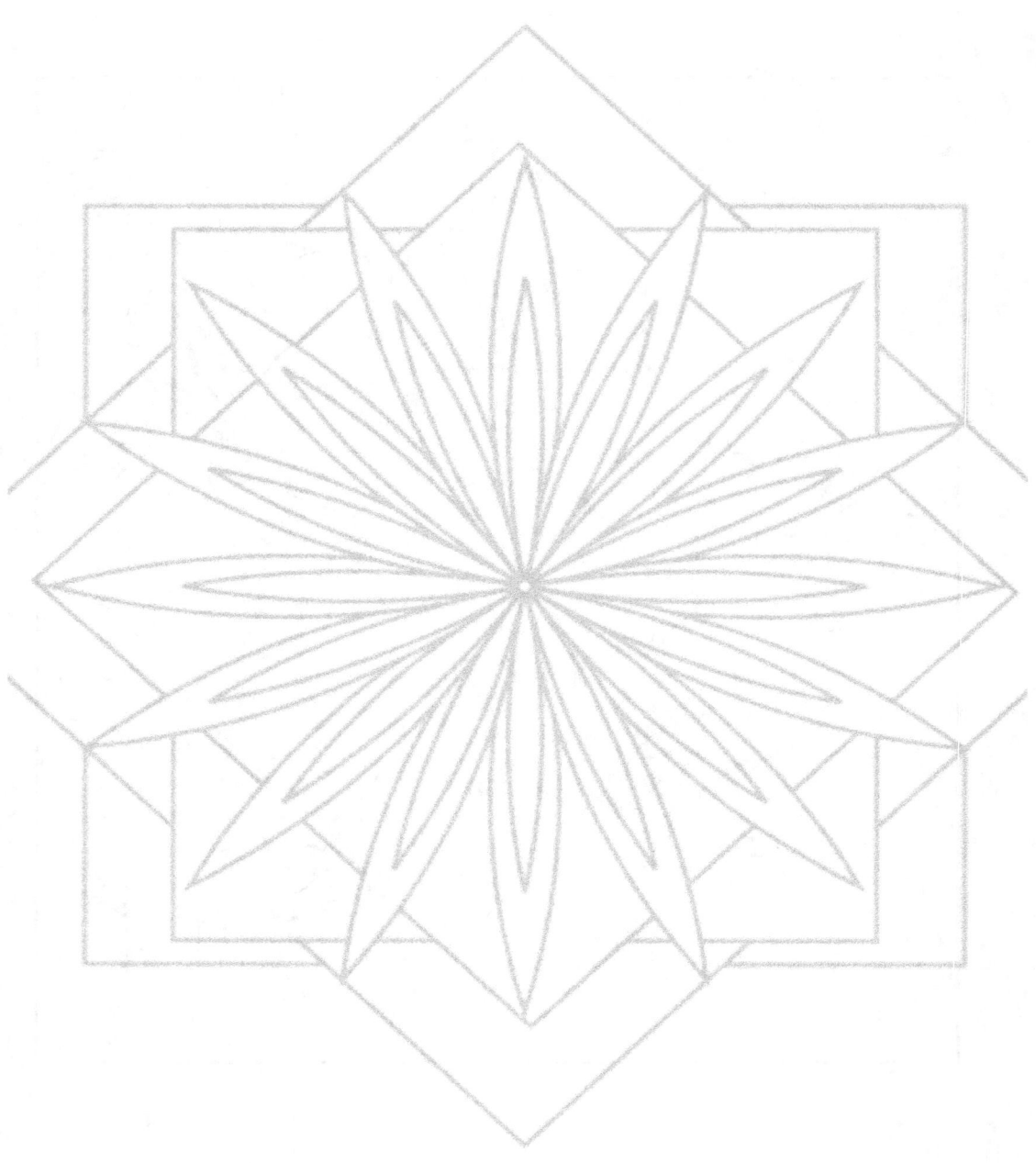

Copyrighted Material

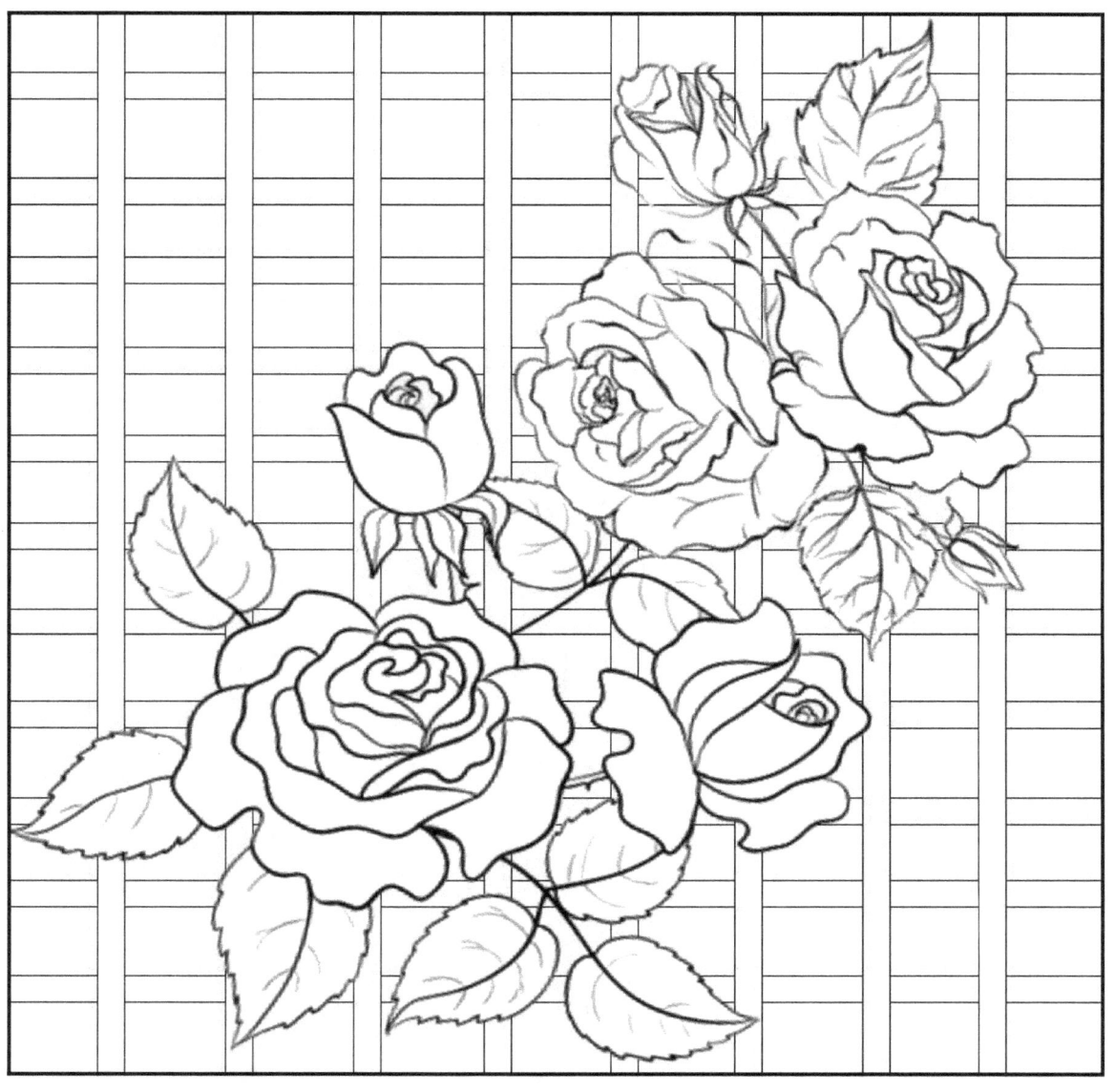

KD Coloring Studio

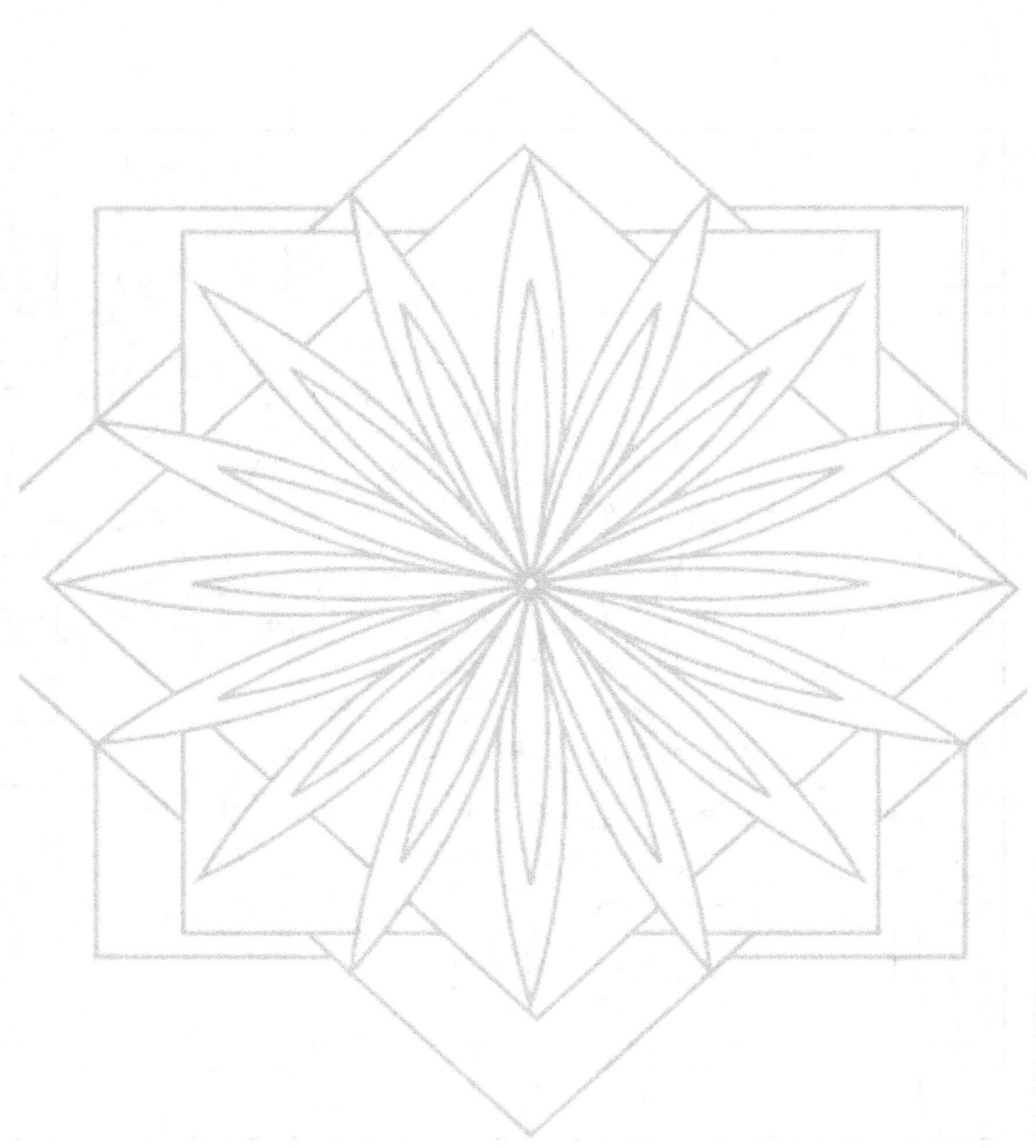

Copyrighted Material

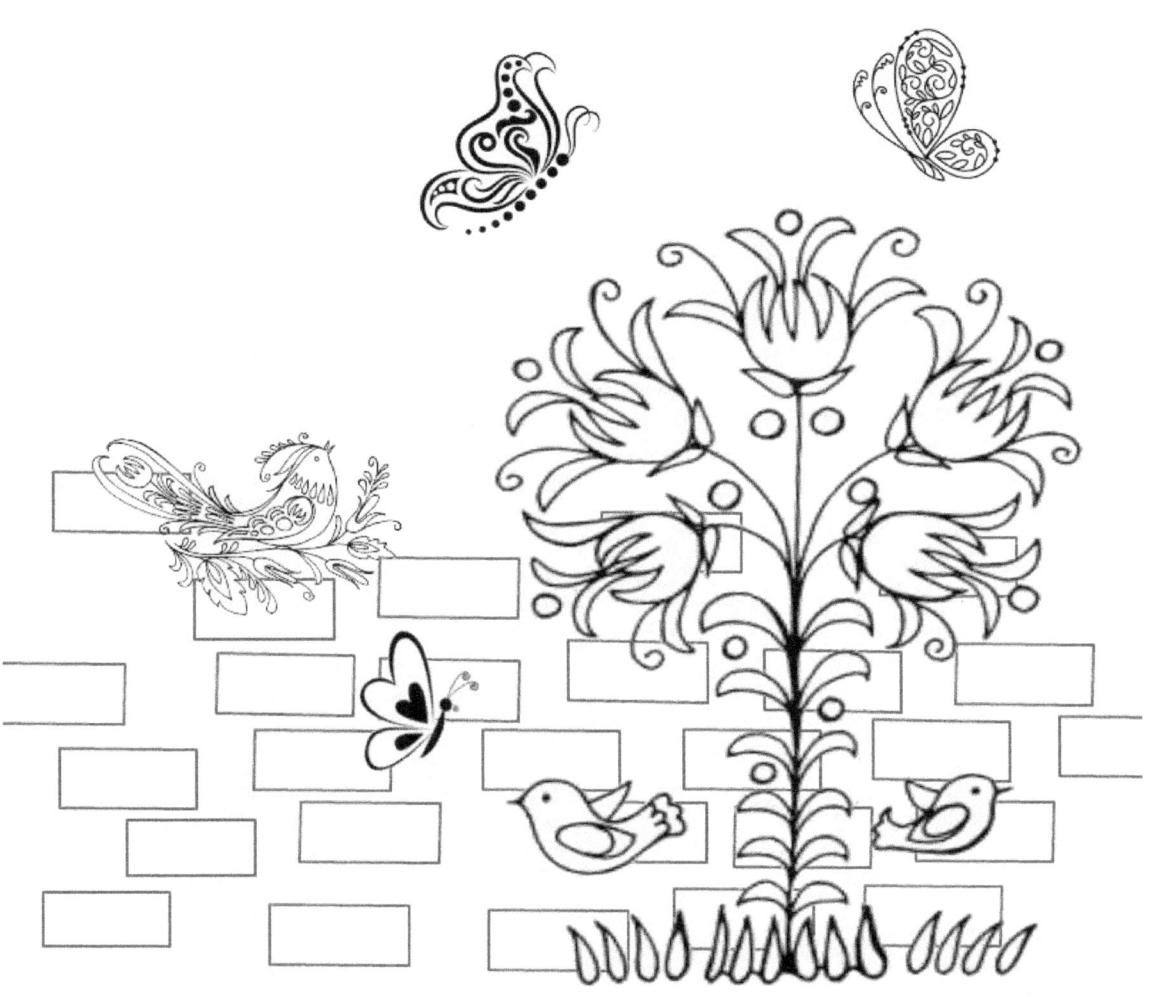

KD Coloring Studio

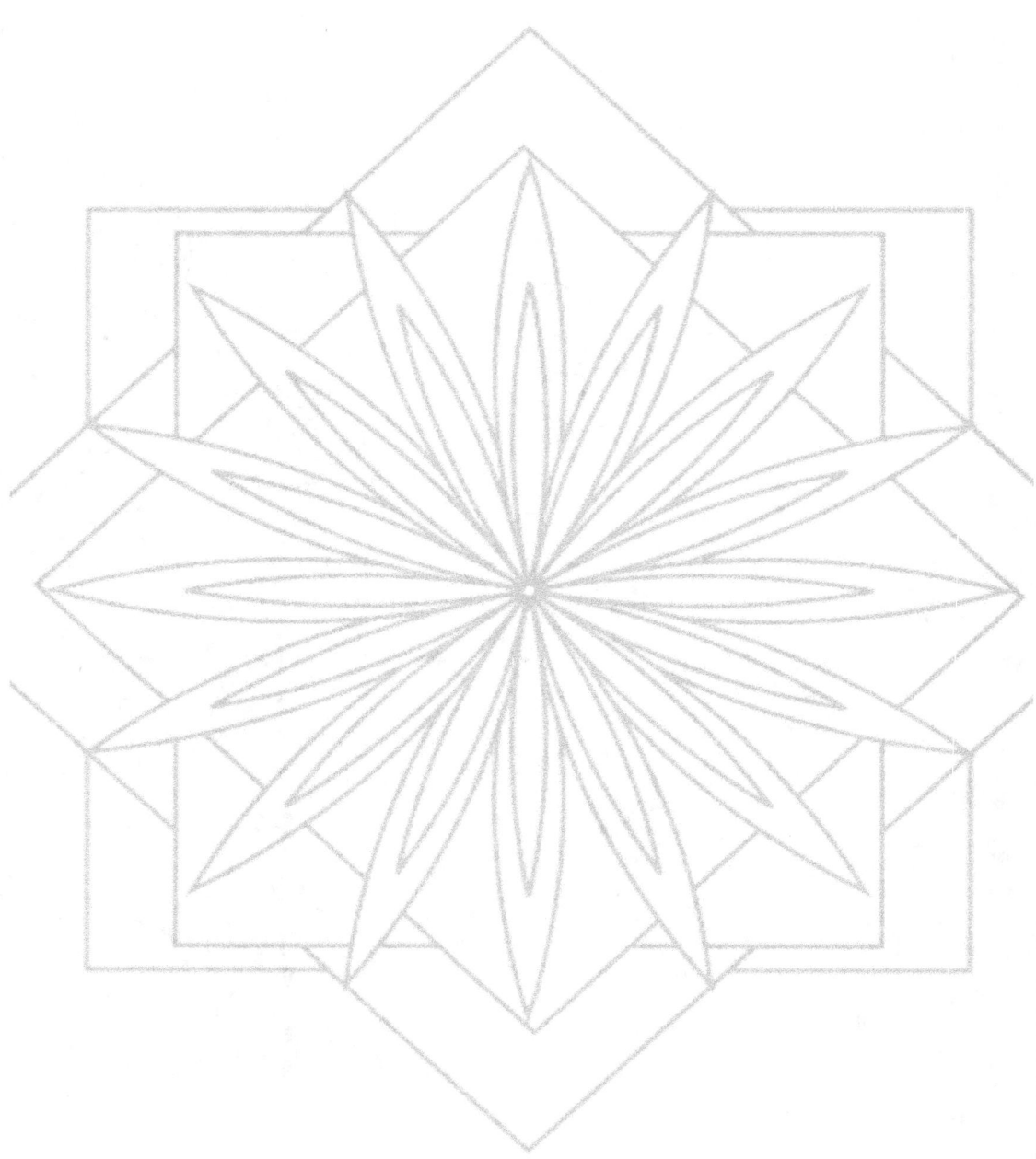

Copyrighted Material

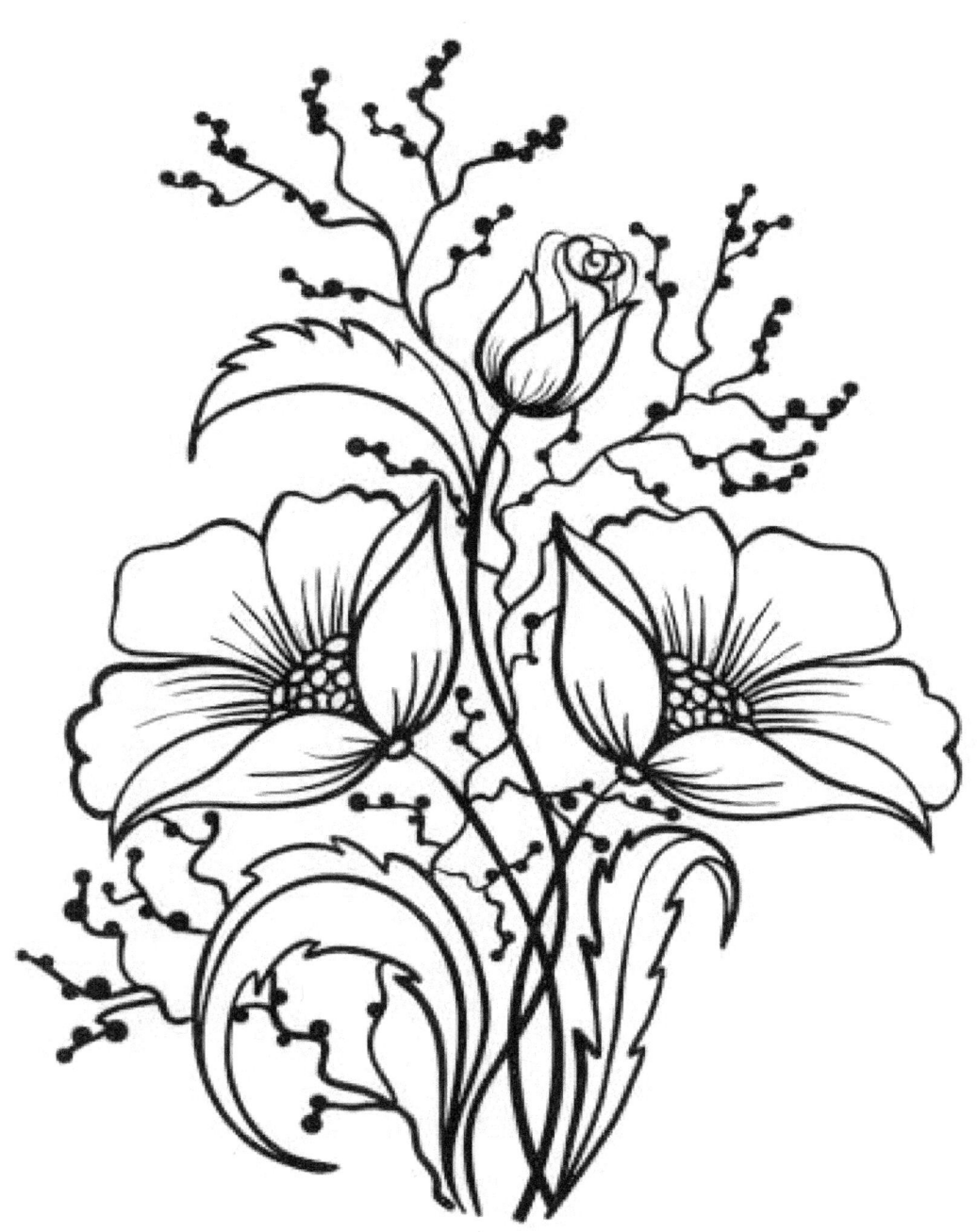

KD Coloring Studio

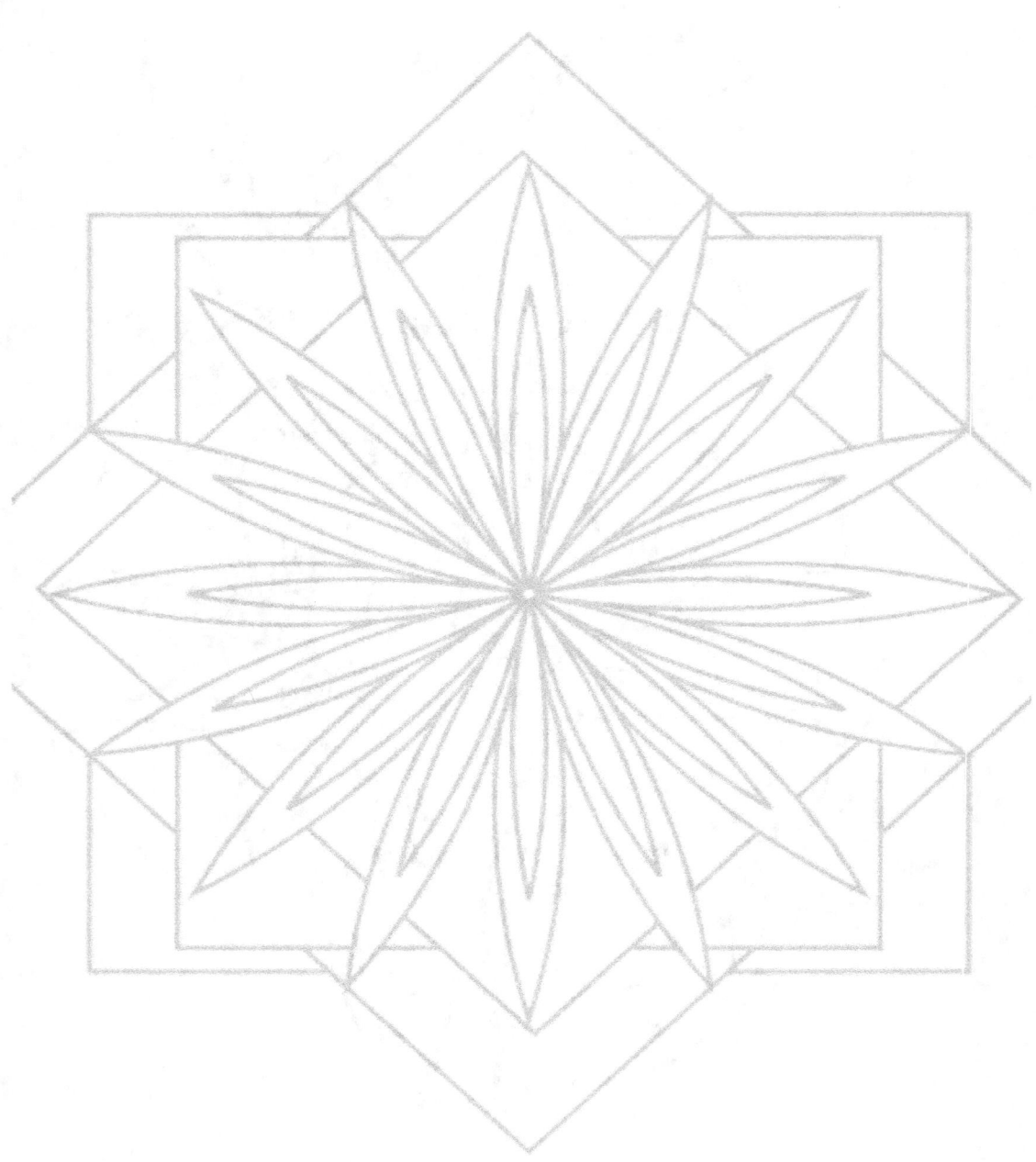

Copyrighted Material

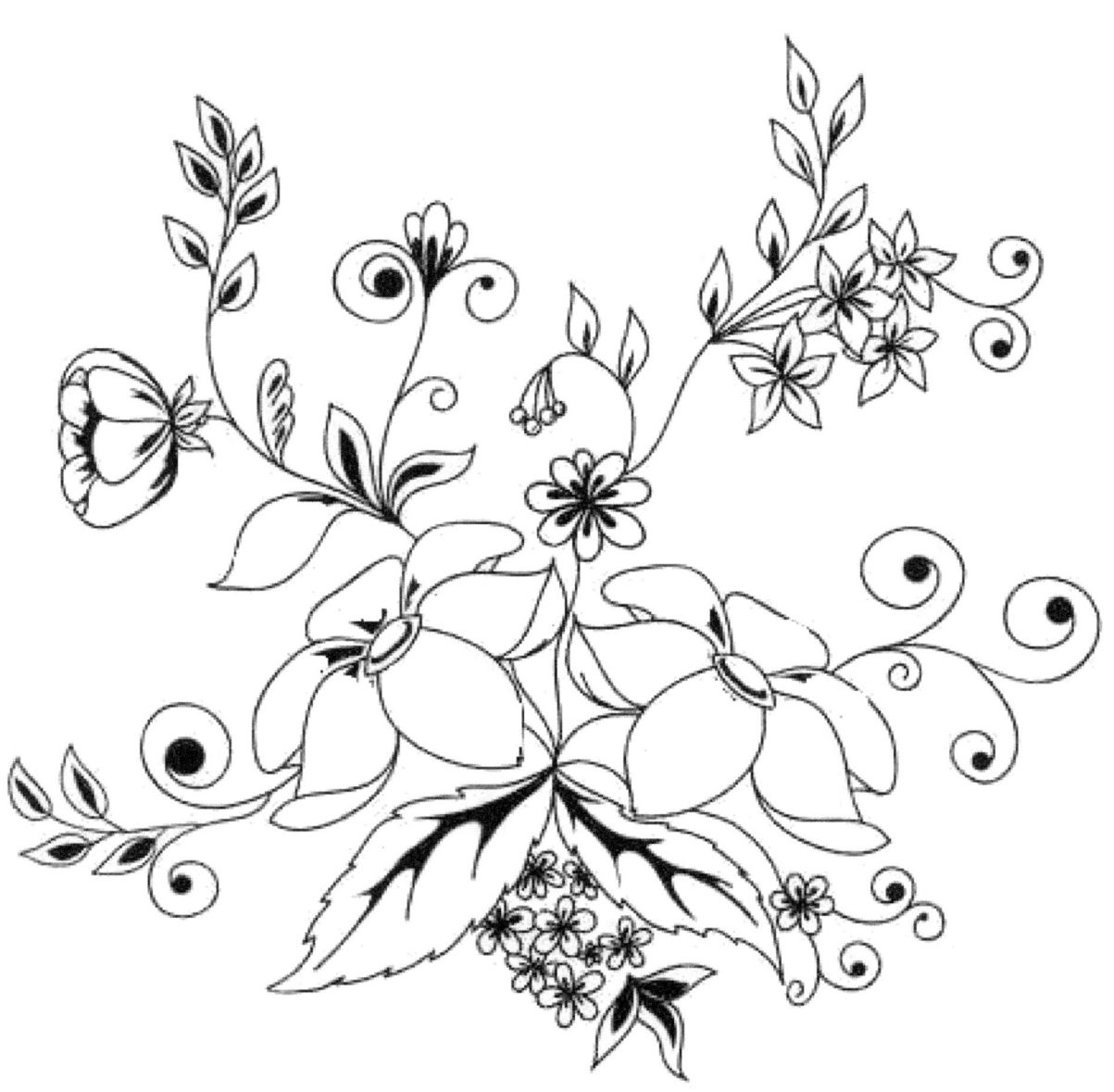

KD Coloring Studio

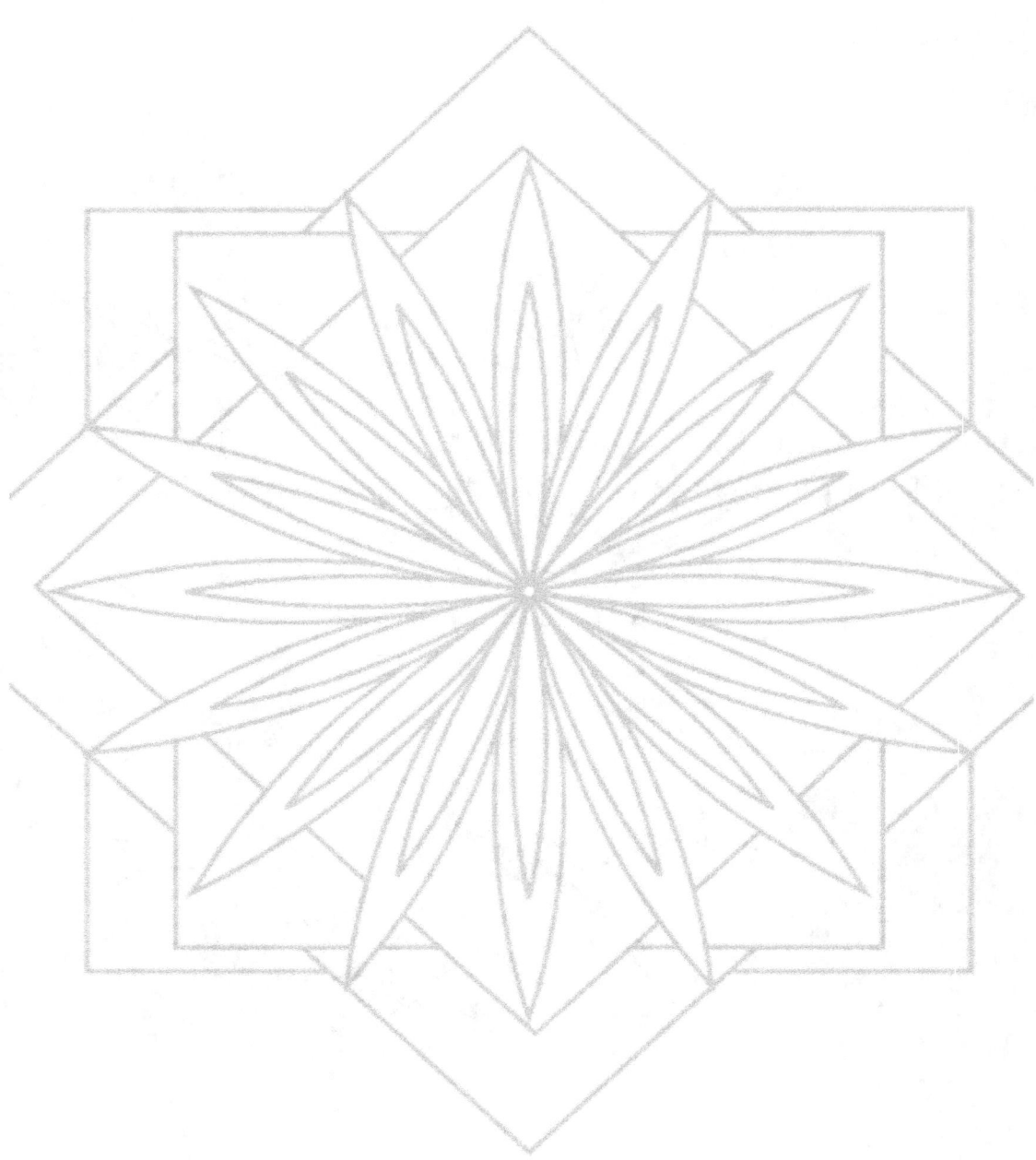

Copyrighted Material

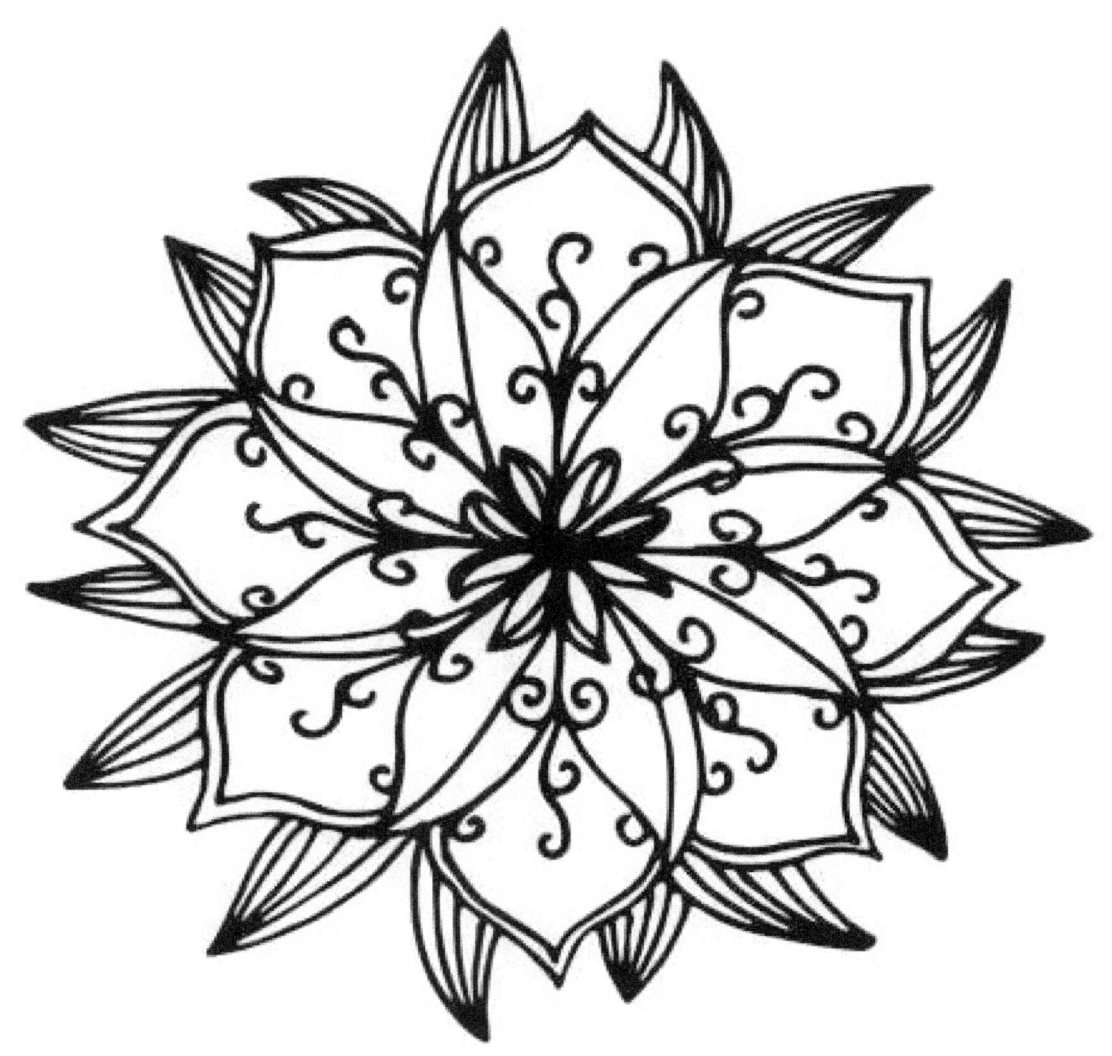

KD Coloring Studio

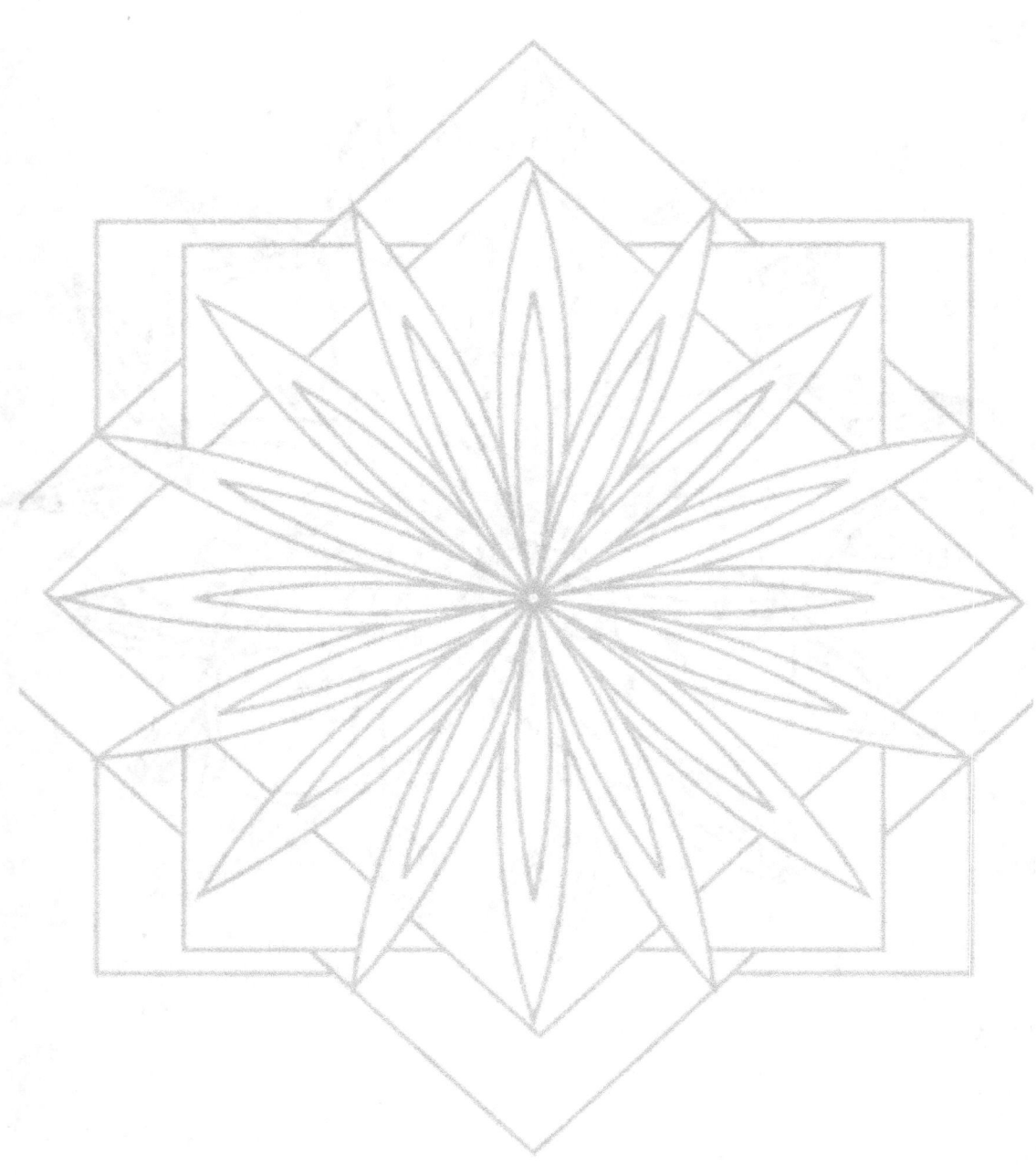

Copyrighted Material

More paperback coloring books can be sourced through

KD COLORING STUDIO AT

http://kdcoloring.com

www.ingramcontent.com/pod-product-compliance
Lightning Source LLC
Chambersburg PA
CBHW080600180526
45168CB00007B/2720